MAHOULISSA

LEGBA

GOU

SEE THE LIGHT THROUGH THE DARKNESS

GREET THE MAGIC, BLACK AND WHITE
FEEL THE CURSE, FEEL THE BLESSING
REVENGE AND SATISFACTION —

VOODOO — MOUNTED BY THE GODS

ALBERTO VENZAGO

INTRODUCTION: WIM WENDERS/ALBERTO VENZAGO
TEXT: ALBERTO VENZAGO/ KIT HOPKINS
FILMSTILLS EDITING UND DESIGN: STUDIO ACHERMANN©

PRESTEL

MUNICH   BERLIN   LONDON   NEW YORK

CONTENTS

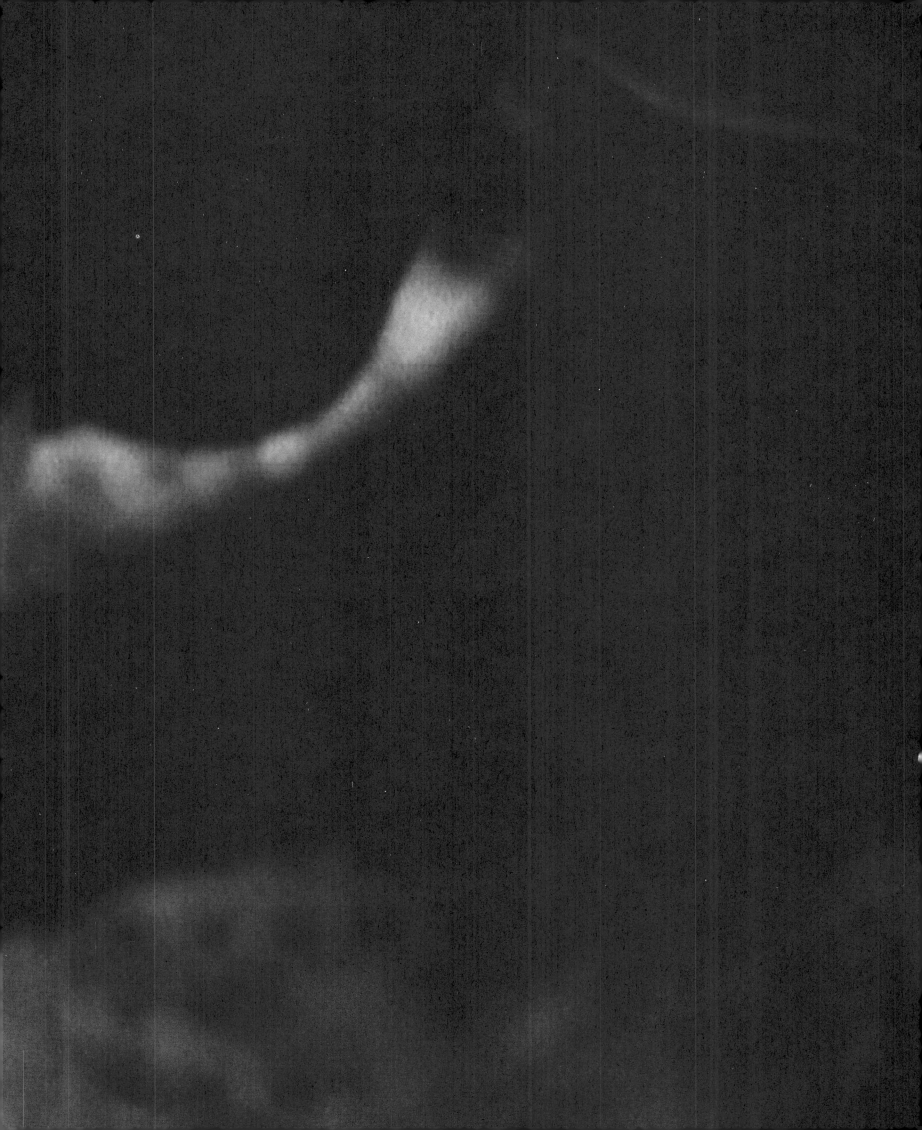

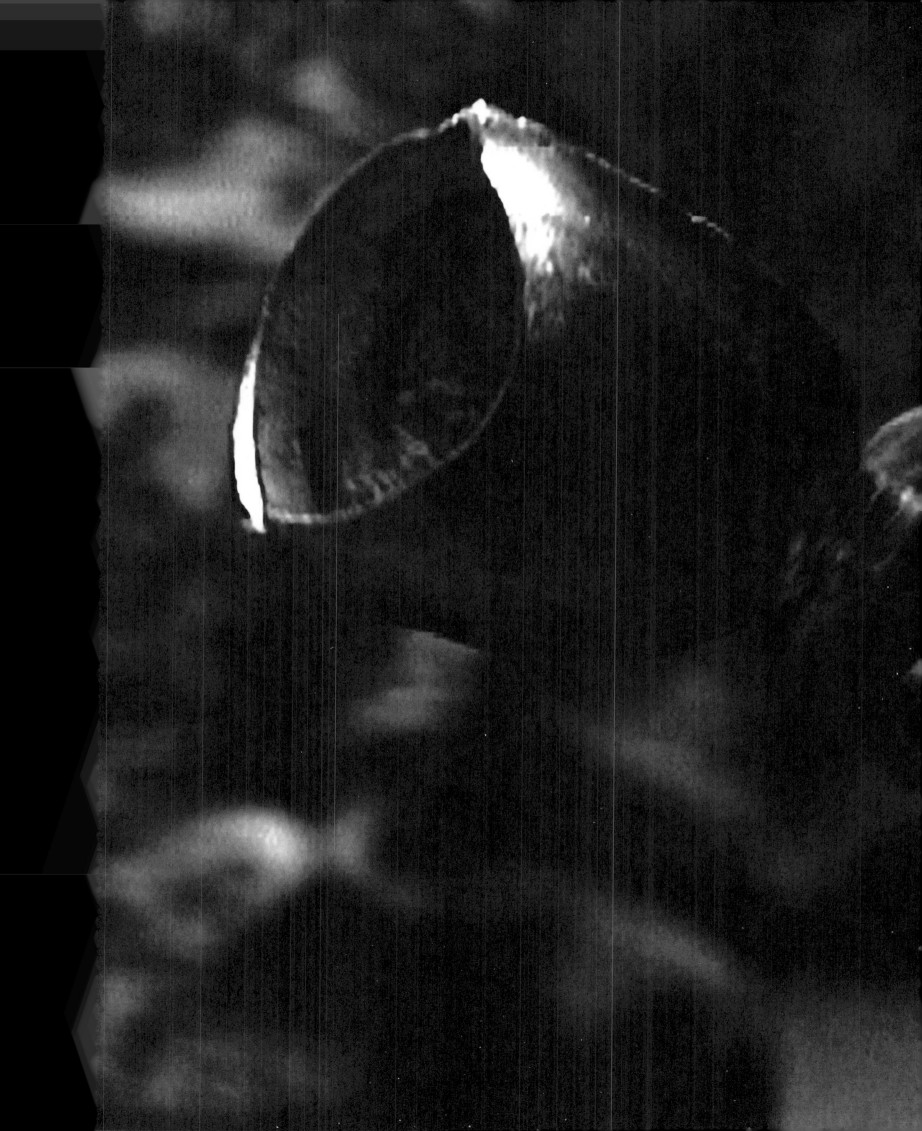

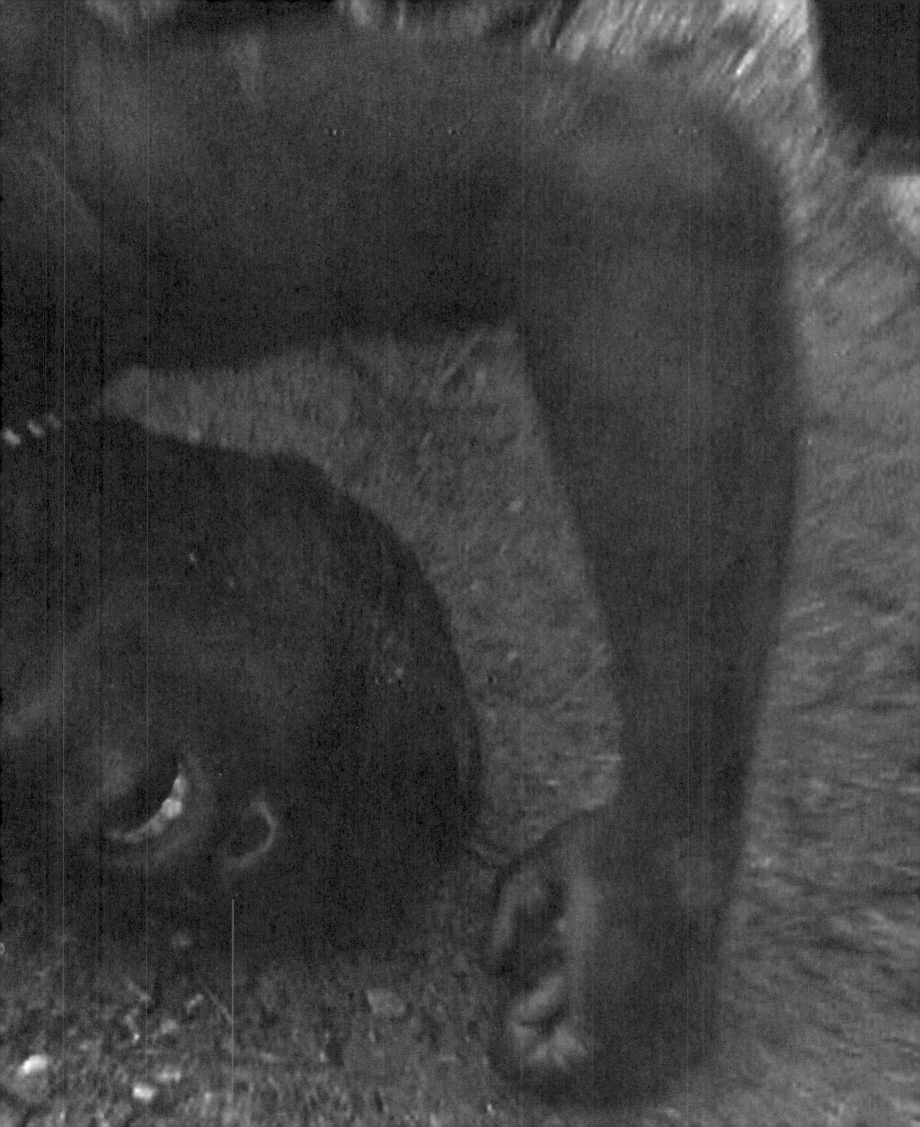

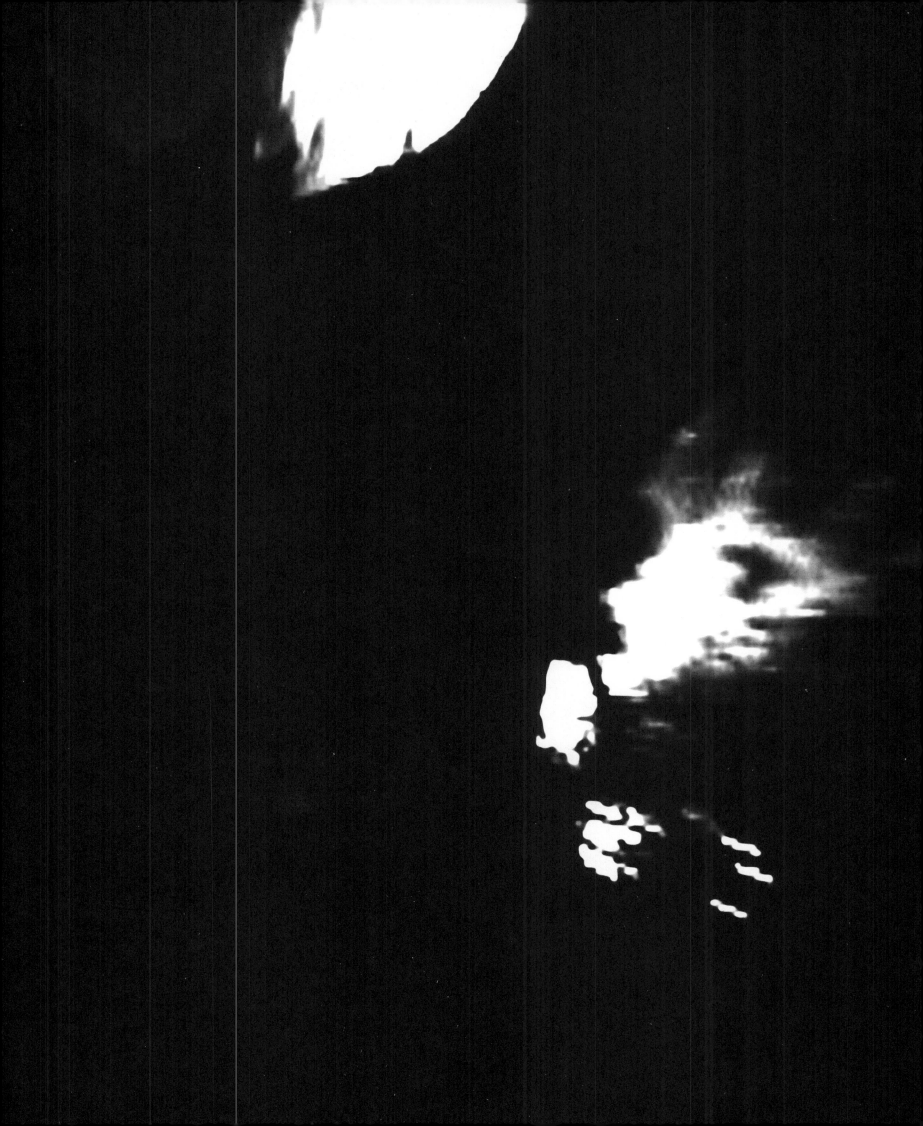

TWO VOICES

~~BLACK AND WHITE~~
WIM WENDERS
ALBERTO VENZAGO

BLACK-AND-WHITE MAGIC

AN INTRODUCTION BY WIM WENDERS

"THE VOODOO MUSIC HAVE EXPECTED THE BOYS TO
JUMP REAL CRAZY AND TO ACT FOR JOY MAKE
THEM THINK LIKE THEY OWN THE WORLD MAKE THEM
THINK THEY ARE CONTROLLING THE GIRLS..."

JB LENOIR

When Alberto Venzago first showed me the as yet unfinished
version of his film <u>MOUNTED BY THE GODS</u>, I spontaneously
dubbed it a 'photographer's film', but I wasn't so sure that he
considered this a compliment (as I certainly intended it to be, as
the film is an absolute photographic masterpiece). And when
I then went on to call this volume of photographs a '<u>BOOK OF
A FILMMAKER</u>', it probably put me firmly into Alberto's bad
books. Perhaps I will succeed, in this introduction,
to make Alberto regard my statements as compliments rather
than paradoxes...

Photography, whether we want it or not, is always in
some way 'selective' in that it illuminates a certain
moment and documents a very specific second in time.
One would be justified in thinking that photographs
showing the world of the voodoo religion would be
fleeting documentations of this nature. At least this is
exactly what one would expect from a photographer
working with the Magnum Photographic Agency. But if
you leaf through this book and immerse yourself in the
extraordinary universe that gradually emerges from
the darkness, quite a different feeling sets in — a definite
sense of permanence! This sequence of pictures
conjures up something that photographs rarely convey:
<u>A SENSE OF TIME!</u>

This extra dimension can really only be achieved through narrative, by introducing a series of fictitious events. But is Venzago telling us a story through the pictures in this book? Aren't the book and film 'documentation'? Or are they 'fabrication' after all? Can we believe our eyes when we watch the film and look at the book? Perhaps we should investigate somewhat more into how the film and photographs came to be made, before we can really 'see the light' through the darkness.

Fifteen years ago, in April 1988 to be exact, Venzago decides to cross the African continent on a Vespa motorbike. The magazine GEO has commissioned him to take photographs. The roads are littered with potholes and sink beneath torrential rain. He has one breakdown after another. In the end, in the town of Ouidah in Benin, the Vespa finally gives up. Alberto photographs the graffiti covered wall where he has come to a standstill. He is not yet aware that a famous voodoo monastery lies behind this very wall, or that the plump, friendly man in flowing garments, who offers the stranded photographer help, is actually Mahounon himself, who presides over this monastery and who is one of the most influential voodoo priests in West Africa. It is not long before Mahounon interprets the oracle for Venzago, and so begins a Swiss man's fascination with voodoo: how can this priest have possibly have known so much about Venzago's past or about his life?

These two very different men become friends. A FEELING OF MUTUAL TRUST DEVELOPS BETWEEN THEM, thus enabling Venzago to start filming two years later, filming which continues throughout THE NEXT TWELVE YEARS. During this period he visits Benin again and again and is allowed to film ceremonies and rituals that no one has ever documented before, and to which no one will probably gain such open access ever again. Alberto managed to make this film 'in the nick of time', CAPTURING THE VERY LAST MOMENT OF INNOCENCE ON THIS particular part of the earth.

And he sees an amazing story unfurl before his eyes: Mahounon foresees his own death a long time before it actually takes place – he is still in full vigor. But he is anxious to find a successor in good time so that he can initiate him into the secrets involved in taking on this post.
Children from all over the country are brought to the monastery, but after a very demanding year as novitiate, none of them are accepted by the Fa, the voodoo oracle. Instead, all signs point to a twelve-year old boy from the neighboring town: GOUNON. Gounon's mother does not want to let her son go to the monastery, and so he is abducted against her will. Venzago films Gounon for four years receiving instruction and being introduced to the mysteries of his religion. From his teacher the boy learns everything that a High Priest should know:

black-and-white magic, ecstatic dances and interpreting the puzzling declarations of the oracle.

As he anticipated, Mahounon dies a sudden and early death. Alberto is there with his camera when Gounon – too young and ill prepared – is faced with the task of following in his master's footsteps. But he survives difficult trials and – at the age of seventeen – he is recognized by all powerful voodoo masters throughout the country. Even the king holds a festive ceremony to welcome him into the circle of High Priests.

The more we get drawn into this story, the more it seems like fiction. From our standpoint it seems like a fairy-tale world far beyond probability. Venzago does not elucidate at all, neither in the film nor in the book. He does not provide us with any ethnological explanations, but just shows what he sees and presents us with phenomena. However, he does not leave us completely alone with the images: they are accompanied by a number of fables and myths from the world of voodoo, related by a powerful narrator whose voice puts the audience under his spell.

The bare facts necessary for understanding the story of Mahounon and Gounon are mentioned almost in passing, but it is mainly these players in this strange, unknown story of creation who enable the audience to penetrate the veil of secrecy that surrounds this religion.

As in the film, the book also recounts these stories, but the effect is completely different. Venzago has succeeded in providing us with a film-like experience as we leaf through these pictures and read the text. As we read on, a sort of rhythm develops which brings the paper alive and which gives the impression that the black-and-white photographs are really beginning to dance. The states of trance depicted seem much more immediate and alive than one would expect from a book of photographs. (In the film he achieves a similar magical effect: color emerges from the world of black and white, and then disappears again without the audience noticing the moment of transition).

But to achieve the same transcendent state of oblivion which one experiences when watching the film, I recommend that you turn up the sound track as loud as possible when you look at the book. Venzago and his musicians, Boris Blank, Peter Scherer, and Jochen Schmidt-Hambrock, have ventured into bold new musical realms; based on real recordings of dances and ceremonies they have created new contemporary music, built up from samples and loops which contain all the flair and whirl of the original music.

At the same time, the music is 'transposed' so that it affects us much more and gets more under our skin than the ethnologically correct sound could probably do. And this is exactly what this work does, this composition of pictures and sound: it gets under our skin! It is impossible to simply dismiss what we have seen and heard. Too much of it is inexplicable, not just the blend of fiction and truth, the pretence interwoven with actual fact, or the juxtaposition of an inflatable Air France Jumbo with ghostly-faced children.

The more I familiarize myself with both the book and the film, the less I feel I know about either of them. So, as you will probably be relieved to hear, Alberto, I would like to retract my original statements. But one thing is quite certain: what you have distilled out of twelve years of incredible experiences, over a hundred hours of video material and thousands of negatives, has never been achieved before, neither in film nor in photography: IT IS UNIQUE IN EVERY SENSE.

WIM WENDERS

PRIVATE OBSESSION, PUBLIC AFFAIR

ALBERTO VENZAGO

ALLADA, ABÉOKOUTA, AFAGNAGAN ... NAMES LIKE A STRING OF PEARLS.
A CHAIN OF TOWNS, EACH JEWEL A VILLAGE. DASSA, SAVINOU,
KILKIBO, PARAKOU, OUIDAH: NAMES OF MINI-STATES AND KINGDOMS.
PEOPLE'S DREAMS. INCLUDING MY OWN.

It's spring 1988. THIS TIME, MY TRIP WOULD HAVE NO DESTINATION. I wanted to experience the other Africa, the Africa of my childhood. I can still smell the yellowing pages of old picture books about explorers, black-and-white engravings of vast primeval forests, animals I'd never seen, rushing torrents and church tower-high waterfalls. I wanted to feel that excitement again. I wanted to plunge into an unfathomable life.

With years of writing reports about the oppressed and the powerful behind me, I'd come to know Africa mainly as an expert in horror. My pictures from the time feature emaciated bodies suffering from starvation, grim-looking despots after the latest military coup or subjects veiled in the transfigured romanticism of the HOMME SAUVAGE. I set off on a Vespa. Bound nowhere in particular. With no time constraints. Simply crossing Africa. LOOKING FOR SOMETHING UNKNOWN.

I found what I was looking for when I was forced to stop. Engine trouble detained me in OUIDAH, a small town in Benin, West Africa. That's how I met Mahounon, one of the highest of voodoo high priests in Africa – for me, the beginning of a long spiritual journey. Of course, at that time it seemed to me to be a pure coincidence. After all, something extraordinary could also have happened in Togo or Ghana or anywhere else on my travels. Or so I thought at the time. Once the kingdom of Dahomey, Benin was A BLACK SPARTA, hemmed in by the Yoruba of modern Nigeria and the Ewe of Eastern Ghana and Togo. According to legend, the royal house of Dahomey goes back to a princess from Adja and a leopard that seduced her on the banks of the Mono. Their kings have sported claw prints on their temples ever since. Dahomey's most-feared warriors were women, and their sole substantial source of income was enslaving and selling subjugated neighboring peoples. When a king died, his successor traditionally went to war to conquer new tribes. It was his duty to increase the nation's wealth.

This strip of land plagued by wars and pillaging raids, later to acquire notoriety as a slave-trading coast, was WHERE THE VOODOO CULT SPRANG UP. Thence it was exported worldwide along with the slaves. When slavery was abolished, Benin lapsed into oblivion. Not endowed by nature with any noteworthy mineral resources (such as oil or diamonds) and geopolitically negligible compared with its much larger neighbors, the country was marginalised, and progress passed it by virtually without trace. A very unspoilt form of life thus survived.

Although opposed by missionaries of all religions and politicians of every color, voodoo remained a firm feature of society.

35% of Benin's population is Christian, 25% Muslim — yet 80% belong to the Voodoo faith. And this figure is due less to statistical error than the admirable tolerance of Africans towards religion.

With the help of <u>MAHOUNON</u>, I immersed myself in another world. He explained monastic life to me and allowed me to participate in well-guarded ceremonies. Above all, it was the innocent naturalness of the people that fascinated me. Since then, I have spent some months there every year.

I had set off on my travels into the unknown without any kind of anthropological background. I really meant to lose my bearings rather than chase after superficial answers, or as one Ghanaian saying goes: <u>"EVEN HEAPS OF WORDS NEVER FILL A BASKET."</u> I feel comfortable with these people. Every visit opens more doors. The unknown becomes better-known, but the longer I stay, the more I think I know the rituals, the more the Voodoosi make me aware I know nothing yet. Trust is not given, it has to be earned. Almost unnoticed, over the years a link has been forged between my two great passions, photography and an interest in rituals. With these, I wanted to try neither to simplify nor to confirm the common place, clichés or half-truths.

One day, Mahounon explained to me that I had not come to Africa for adventure; he had brought me there to document his life story. Maybe so — the result is twelve years of work. Out of it came a film, a CD and this book.

It's high summer when I take part in Mahoumon's burial ceremonies. It's pitch-dark in the burial chamber. As I measure the meagre light, the high priests begin the ceremony. Stooping to the sound of drumbeats, they slowly retreat into the burial chamber with a goat and a chicken, while the monastic community outside dances and sings in the stifling heat. I'm just about to begin filming when Kpassenon and the priests of the NEW MAHOULISSA CULT hand me a fetish. For nine years I've been just a journalist. I never crossed the narrow line dividing observer from participant. And apart from Pierre Verger, no white man has become a FATUMBIE — a voodoo priest, an initiate, an insider. I'm now part of the ceremony. Filming is just incidental. Mahonounon's prophecy has come to pass. Gounon has been installed as his successor. Mobile phones and TV sets have irrupted into this unspoilt world. Ouidah has changed fast as have its inhabitants. But the friendship has not been sundered with the completion of the film and the book. It remains intact.

THIS IS NOT A TEXTBOOK. IT'S AN INVITATION TO A JOURNEY:

A journey to the origins of voodoo, and Kpassenon, the guardian of the sacred grove, and Aboli Ahgbo, the king in Abomey with his forty-two wives; to Fofo the magician, who punishes unpleasant rivals telepathically with a permanent erection, and to Gounon, who at the age of twenty-one has to bear the burden of the whole monastic community; to a landscape still untouched by tourist hordes; to people of profound devoutness.

My thanks are due to all my friends in Ouidah, particularly my production manager Lambert Abagadan, who showed me an Africa that's more than a picture from childhood days. To artist Yves Pede, translator Martine de Souza, my friend and Voodosi Gounon Tokpo, Kpassenon, guardian of the sacred grove, who calls me 'mon prince', Fofo, and Mahounon's whole family. They all find room in my heart.

I must express particular gratitude to Thilo Röscheisen, who not only freely gave me ideas and texts during this project but stood by me as a friend with advice and practical help. My thanks also to Kit Hopkins for her years of support and inspiration since the beginning of my obsession. She turned the legends and stories I wrote down like a hunter and collector into wonderful texts in the film and the book.

I made friends not only in Africa. Wim and Donata Wenders also entered my life. I'm grateful and happy they're there. Wim supported the project as executive producer and gave me confidence in the power of pictures.

The book is finished. 125 photographs, generally taken at 1/125th of a second. In all, that makes a second. <u>A SECOND IN OUIDAH – A SLICE OF TIME</u>. But what does time mean in Africa? 'Il y a trois jours' (three days ago), Mahounon used to say, even if we'd not seen each other for a whole year.

ALBERTO VENZAGO

THE DARKNESS

~~"HELP ME! HELP ME!", THEY BEG~~
~~"WHY ARE YOU CRYING", ASKED LEGBA~~

"WHY ARE YOU CRYING?" ASKED LEGBA.
"MY FATHER IS DEAD AND I LOST MY GUIDE.
IM ALONE AND I DON'T KNOW WHAT WILL BECOME
OF ME," MOANED
                    THE PRINCE

WHY

PEOPLESCAPE

¬ THE ABIKOUS OF DJOHITIN

If a woman has a miscarriage, she must go to the Abikous for advice. A quantity of fabric is offered up.
When she then becomes pregnant and bears a healthy child, she must bring the baby back
to the <u>ABIKOUS</u>. They will cut a scar on one of its cheeks. Every year from that time, the mother will bring
money, food, even a whole goat. If this is not done, the mother will have problems.

The Abikous are considered very dangerous. The villagers live in fear that they will be spoken
to by them: "Help me! My clothes are old and soiled. Help me!" they beg.

Abikous have very high voices, and speak in either Fon or Yoruba.
They are only allowed to go out during the day. <u>THEY HAVE NO RIGHT TO THE DARKNESS</u>.

THE DARKNESS

THE ACHINA VOODOOSIS

visit Mahounon's Mahoulissa monastery and wait to convey their good wishes to Gounon, and give him strength. (Achina is <u>THE GRAIL</u> of Voodoo).

¬ T H E   G E N E S I S   L E G E N D

There descended once upon our land a time of darkness and chaos. Fires destroyed our forests,
the oceans went wild, and the heavens forgot how to make rain. Pregnant women gave birth to goats,
not babies. Water holes dried up, the ground became like stone.
There was no harvest. Mothers went mad watching their children die of hunger. Fights broke out
among our people.
Everyone looked for SOMEONE TO BLAME FOR THE DISASTERS. The elders gathered, desperate for
a solution. They found none. And the suffering continued.

One day a woman appeared in our midst from the land of Adja.
She was A WISE WOMAN, guided by two leopards. She looked upon our land of chaos and darkness
and told our king:

Your suffering will end only when you worship, as we do, THE GODS OF VOODOO.

¬ T H E   M A H O U L I S S A   L E G E N D

Man-woman Mahoulissa, the Supreme God and ruler of the heavens. One being with two faces.
The first face is female, and its eyes are the moon. The second is male, and its eyes, the sun.
Mawu directs the night, and Lissa, the day.
SINCE MAHOULISSA IS BOTH MAN AND WOMAN, she became pregnant. She divided the universe
among her many children: the earth went to the eldest, the heavens to her twins, the oceans
to her third-born, and so on.
But there was nothing left for her youngest child, the spoiled favorite, Legba. So she made him
her messenger. He alone can speak with all beings, earthly and heavenly.
He can be cruel and mischievous. The key to Legba's good will is sacrifice. BLOOD SACRIFICE.

¬ L E G B A S I

It is the job of this young Voodoosi to keep the audience entertained
at the three-day Legbasi celebration. The <u>COLA NUTS</u> she has in her mouth will be bitten
into sixteen pieces and used to read <u>THE FA, THE VOODOO ORACLE</u>.

THE   WOODEN   DOLLS

represent twins related to the Voodoosi who have died, usually at birth.

The Voodoosi then carries the doll, or dolls, with her, in which <u>THE SIBLING'S SPIRIT LIVES</u>, day and night.

She knows that if she ever forgets or loses the doll,

something terrible will happen to her. The doll has to do everything she does.

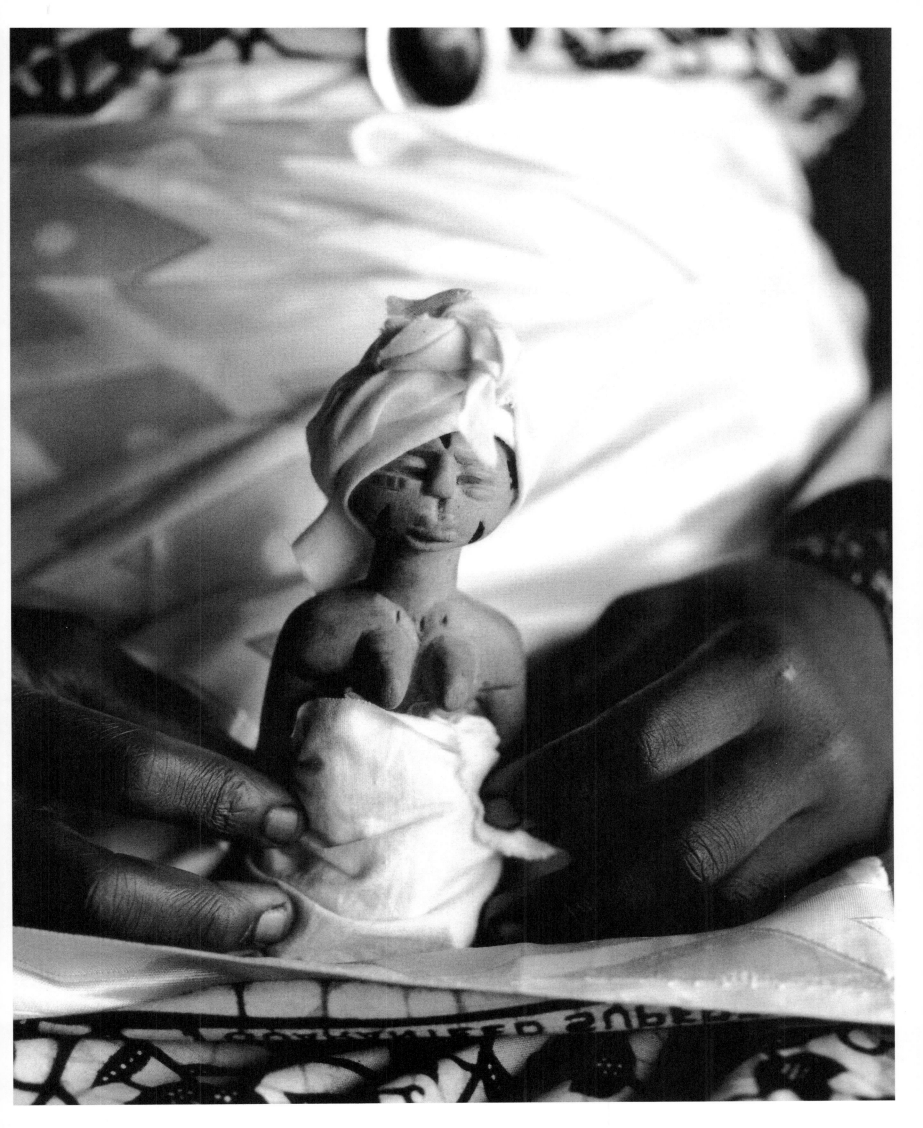

¬ THE WOODEN DOLLS II

When the time comes for an initiation ceremony, the dolls are dressed in tiny ceremonial costumes
and are initiated too. If the child dies, no one would ever say she was dead.
It would be said that she had disappeared into the sacred forest, <u>SEARCHING FOR HER TWIN</u>.

¬ THE BIG CEREMONY

High priest Mahounon at the lavish three-day celebration announcing Gounon as his successor.

Voodoo dignitaries from all over Benin have come to pay their respects.

VISIT TO LIMBO
¬ L O O K I N G   I N W A R D

A patient at a Benin mental asylum in Cotonou digging a hole in which he intends to hide.
He went into a trance and never came out of it. The institution has bungalows for 150 patients.
They look inward to a world to which we have no access.

THE DARKNESS

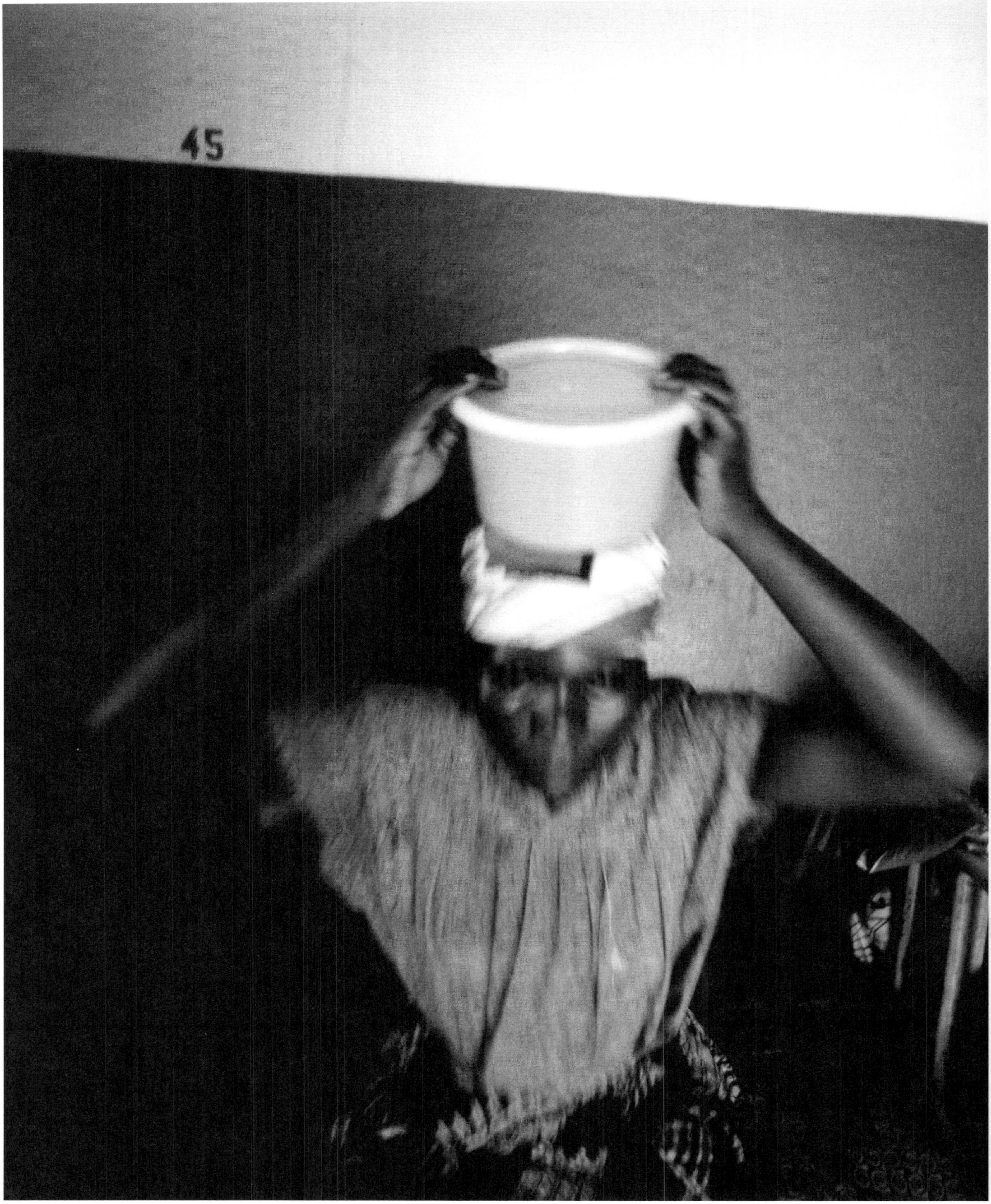
45

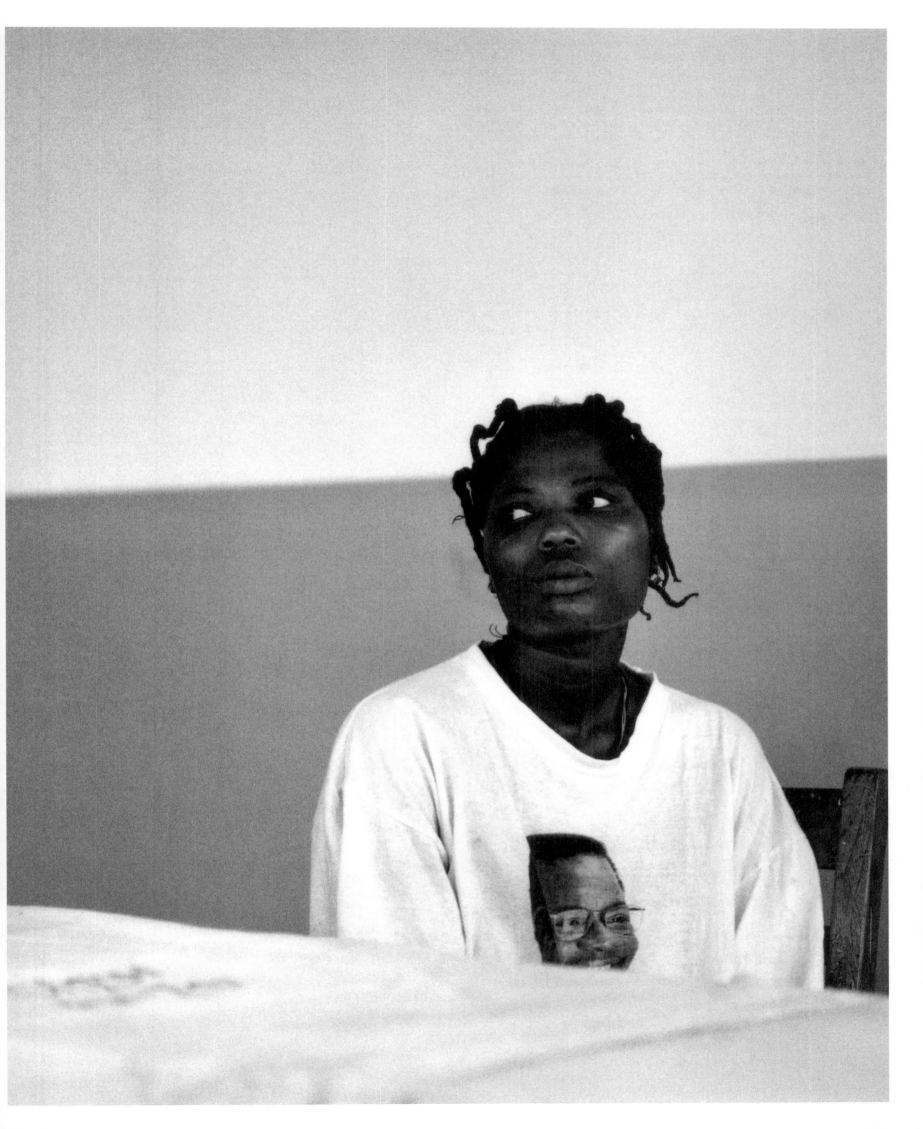

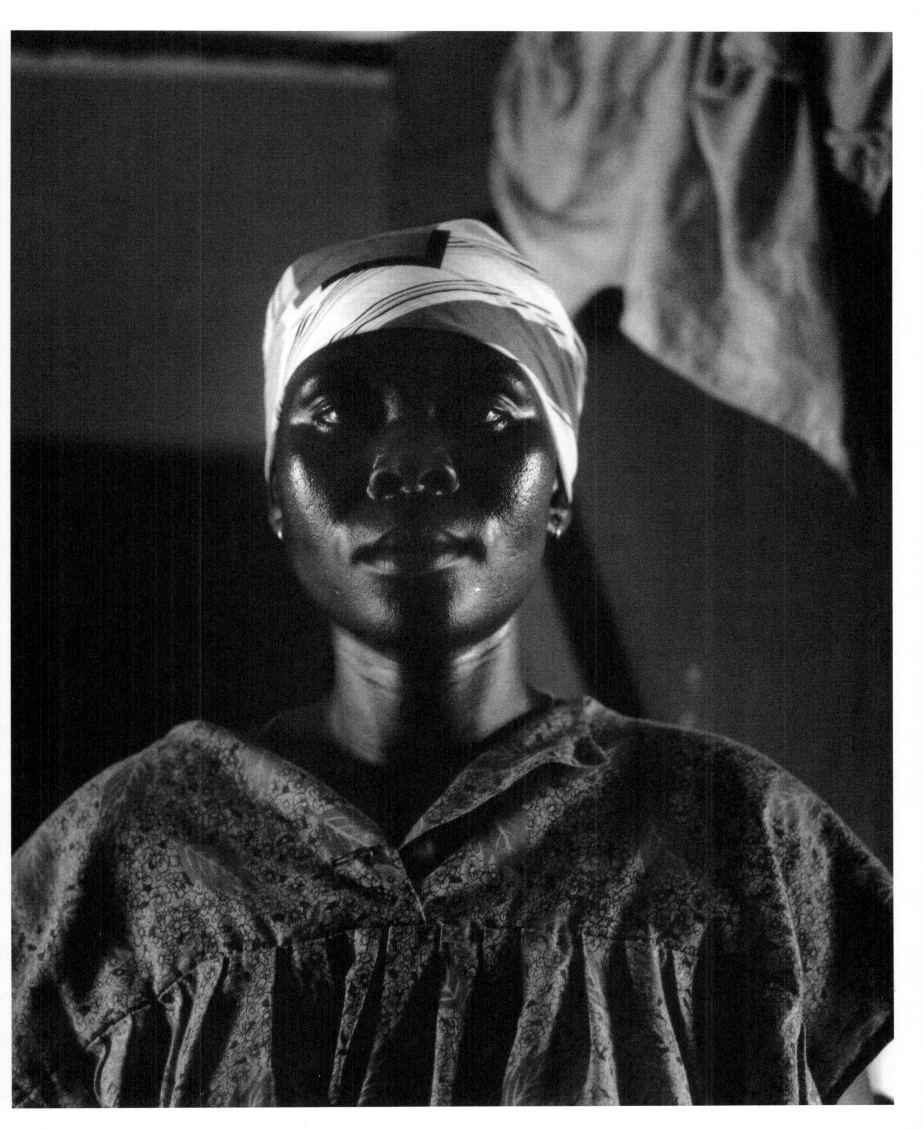

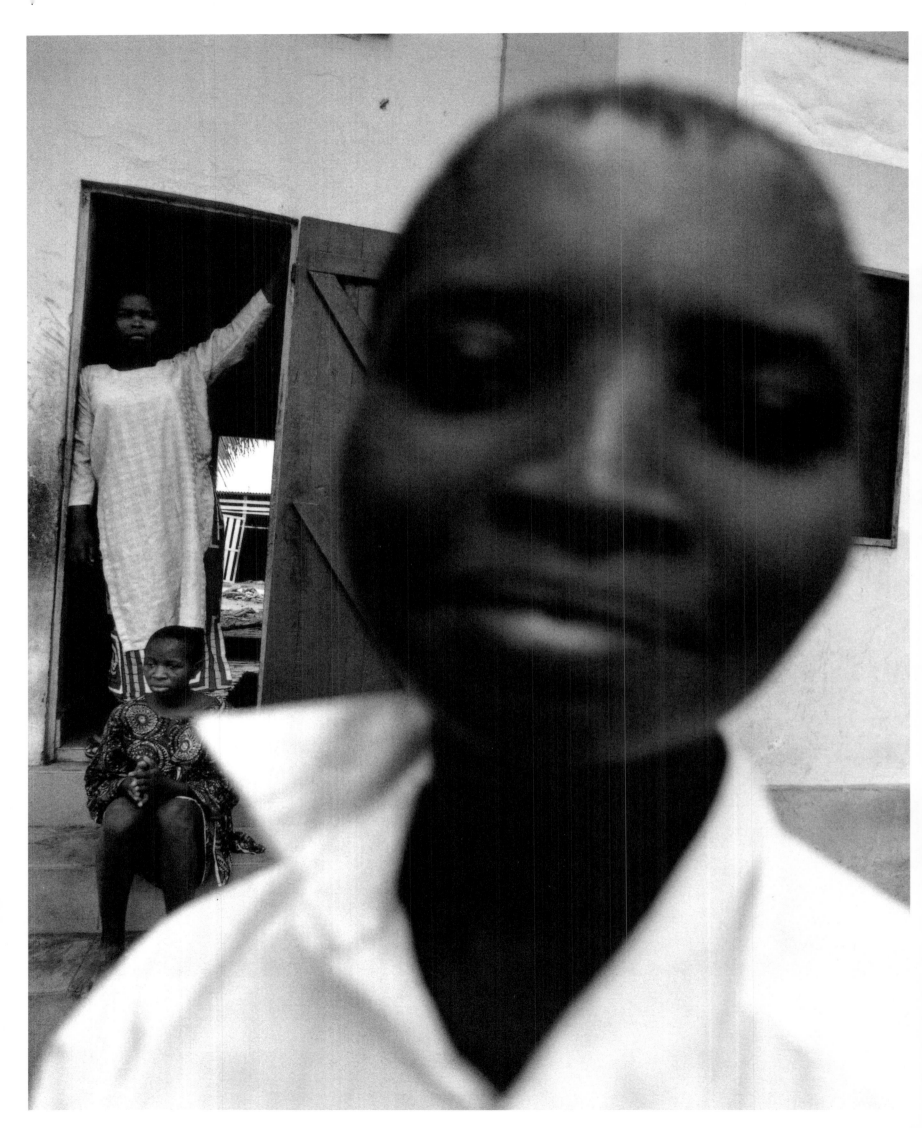

🯅

¬ L E G B A

T H E   T R I C K S T E R

One day, <u>THE SUPREME GOD, MAHOULISSA</u>, heard in the heavens the loud sobbing of a man-child.
Touched by his grief, she sent her son, Legba, to console him.

<u>LEGBA</u> followed the sobs until he came to the palace. He found a young prince weeping in the dark.
"Why are you crying?", asked Legba. "My father is dead and I lost my guide.
   <u>I AM ALONE AND I DON'T KNOW WHAT WILL BECOME OF ME</u>," moaned the boy.

"What will you give me if I find you someone who will guide you and care for you forever,
as long as you live?" queried Legba. "All my jewels," replied the prince.
Legba took the boy by the hand and led him outside into the sunlight. He pointed to the ground.
"There. <u>THERE IS YOUR GUIDE</u>. Now give me your jewels."

         The prince objected: "But that's my shadow! It's mine! And it was always there! It's me!"
"Exactly," said Legba, grabbing the prince's crown and scepter, and scampering away.

MAGICIANS & SORCERERS

¬ C H A K A T O U S

Chakatous, or sorcerers, have their vocation made clear to them by a significant, even extraordinary event in their lives. Cosmé, for example, was working as a conductor on a Benin train. There was a terrible crash and he was the only survivor. He knew this meant he HAD BEEN CHOSEN to execute the will of the gods.

Ceremonies conducted by the chakatous REQUIRE GREAT PREPARATION.

All the ingredients can be purchased at the fetish market.

THE DARKNESS

¬ S M O K E

For the chakatous, smoke is considered a source of strength and power.

❝

¬ M A H O U ' S   W A Y S   A R E   J U S T

Traveling the earth, Legba met a man who became his companion. He did not know that Legba was a god.
The two of them spent the night at a family's home. Their child was very ill.
Legba gave some powder to the father to give to the sick child, then hurried back to his companion.
"Quick, quick! We must leave!" As they were running away from the house, they heard the family shouting,
"Where is the stranger?" <u>THE CHILD WAS DEAD</u>.

The next night they took shelter in another house. At dawn, Legba took some flint and made a fire.
He set fire to the straw house where he had slept. He hurried over to his companion: "Wake up!
We must go! Hurry!" As they left, the house burst into flames. The people cried: "Where are the strangers
who did this?"

The companion was ashamed of what Legba had done and tried to run away. Legba caught him.
"You are astonished at what I have done. I am not a human being, <u>I AM LEGBA</u>,
<u>THE GOD, SON OF MAHOULISSA</u>. She sent me to do what I have done. If I had not destroyed that child,
it would have killed its own parents before it was grown. The family where I burned the
house had many rich relatives. But they were greedy and wouldn't share their wealth with the children.
When they begin to build the foundations anew, the children will find the hidden money."

"When, in the course of life you see such things, know that it is <u>MAHOULISSA'S DIVINE WILL</u>."

¬ L E G B A

A shrine dedicated to the god, Legba, moulded at the entrance of a house to keep
it safe from disease, evil spirits and death. Legba serves as the link between the gods
of Voodoo and men. **NOTHING CAN BE DONE WITHOUT HIS CONSENT** and he
is often fickle and cruel.

GRIS-GRIS & ASSINS

F E T I S H E S

are __THE SACRED OBJECTS__ used by healers and sorcerers to communicate with the gods.

Each of the believers' houses has a room devoted to the dead. It's filled with altars, or assins, each dedicated to an ancestor. The dead are to be cherished and respected, not feared. They can guide and protect us.

A cross added to an assin indicates the conversion of the ancestor to Christianity.

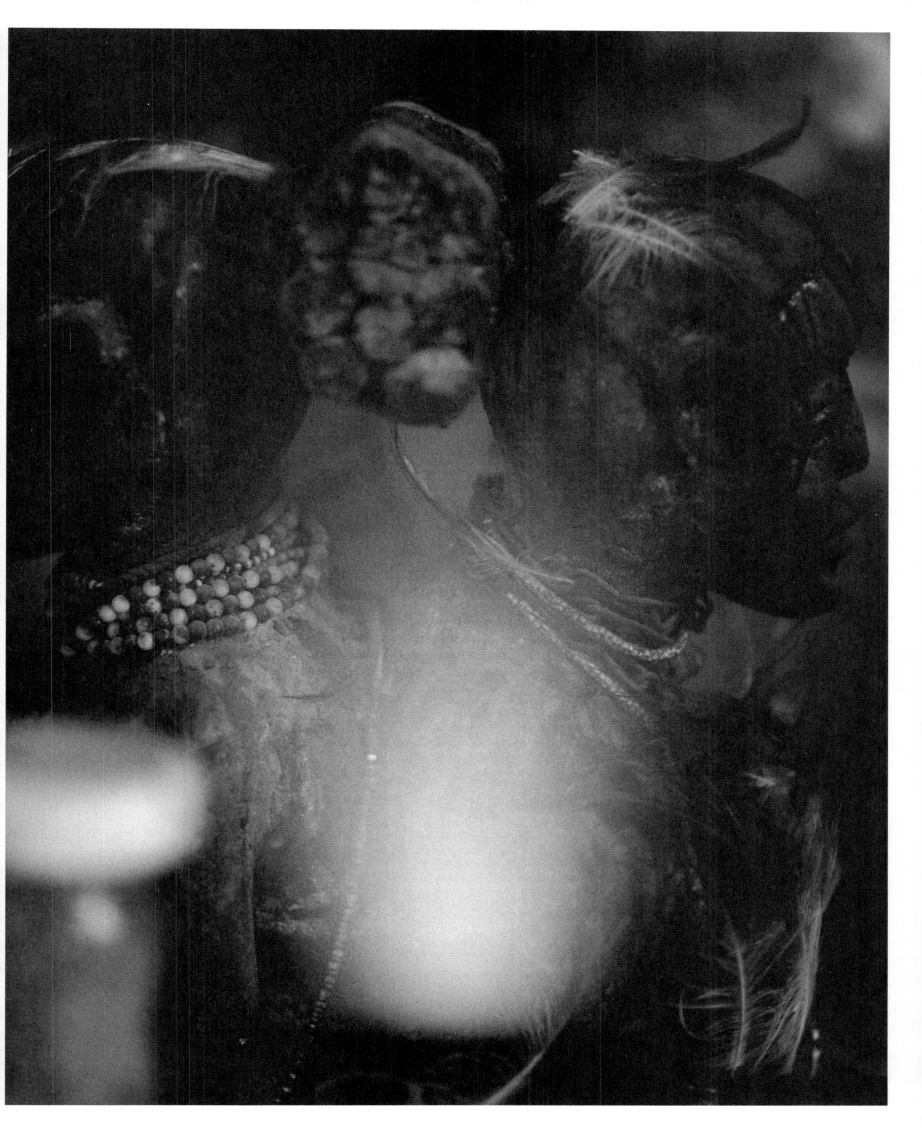

Daniel Avoudjeman of Agonssa, Ouida using a fetish to <u>CAST A SPELL</u>.
The god Legba must approve all dealings between mortals and deities.

¬ L E G B A   T R I C K S   M A H O U L I S S A

For a time, <u>THE SUPREME GOD, MAHOULISSA AND HER SON, LEGBA</u>, lived together on earth. Whenever anything good happened, people thanked Mahoulissa, even if Legba was responsible. Whenever anything went wrong, she blamed it on her son. The people began to hate Legba.

Mahoulissa had a garden in which she planted yams. Legba told her that thieves were planning to steal them all. So Mahoulissa gathered all the people on earth to tell them that the first one who stole from her garden would be killed.

It rained that night. Legba went to Mahoulissa's house and stole her sandals. He put them on, went to the garden, and stole all the yams. In the morning the theft was discovered. At once Legba insisted that all the people assemble to see whose feet fit the footprints in the mud. Although all the people came, they did not find anyone whose foot matched the print.
Now Legba said: "Is it possible that Mahoulissa herself came at night and has forgotten it?"
Mahoulissa protested that this was absurd, but agreed to measure her foot against the print. It matched perfectly. The angry crowd cried, "<u>HERE IS AN OWNER WHO IS HERSELF A THIEF!</u>"

Mahoulissa was humiliated. She knew her own son had tricked her. She ascended far away into the heavens, away from the troubles of earth, <u>LEAVING THE CUNNING LEGBA TO HIS OWN DEVICES</u>.

TELEPHONE
FERTILITY
HOHO
PROTECTION
THE DIVINING

~~THE DOLLS~~

THE FETISHES

¬ T H E   T E L E P H O N E

In order to communicate with the gods, custom-made telephones are used. They are made out of a bottle with a statue inside, representing the owner of the phone. No one is expected to question how the statue got into the bottle.

¬ M A K I N G   T H E   C A L L

A large cowrie shell is glued to the bottle's neck. Scraps of red fabric (usually from an article of the owner's clothing), are wrapped around the base. Two smaller cowries are attached, one to the left and one to the right.

In order to address a prayer to the divine, some drops of your own perfume have to be put in the bottle on the day you wish to communicate. The bottle is then held with both hands, the thumbs pressing against the two cowrie shells on the base. The lips are then positioned against the large cowrie shell on the neck and the wish made in a whisper.

THE FETISHES

¬ THE   CARRIER
OF   THE   MESSAGE

The bochio has a hole in its stomach into which the
Bokounon whispers the supplicant's prayer. It can be good
or bad: a curse for revenge, for example, or a wish
for fertility. After he has whispered the message into the
hole, the Bokounon replaces the peg. It is at this
point that the magic goes into effect. At the bottom of
the bochio is a metal spike which can be driven into the
ground. DEPENDING UPON THE NATURE OF THE
MESSAGE, the bochio is placed in an appropriate
location. This can be on a secluded path leading to the
market, in a field or in a Fa consultation room, for
example. Sometimes they are placed secretly under a bed
or in a special box or trunk.

THE EMPOWERED CADAVER

is heavily laden with small packets containing substances of religious potency. These are bound to the figure by various means such as beads, leather, and string. Although much of the figure is hidden under its load, it emanates a strong sense of immobility, of stillness. It is one of the smaller fetishes, but certainly one of the most powerful. A glance under its skirt shows the statue to be generously endowed indeed.

¬ G I F T S   O F   G O O D   F O R T U N E

The Hoho here do not represent children, but deities. When twins are born, they are considered to be a promise of good fortune for the parents. Because they occur so rarely, twins receive special treatment and are guided by strict rules. They must share everything equally between them.

IF ONE TWIN DIES, a small statue is carved to take its place. The mother carries it around with her at all times. After a period of time, the surviving twin takes over the care of the statue. He shares his food with it and has it dressed in clothes identical to his own.

Twins are not necessarily represented as identical. Sometimes one is smooth and polished, the other rough and crude. EVEN IF ONLY ONE IS BORN MAGIC, its supernatural character spills over to the second twin.

THE FETISHES

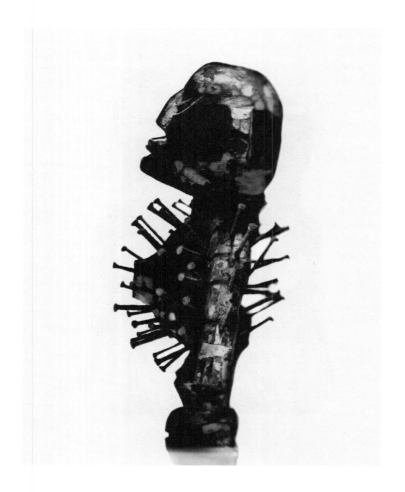

The fetish as a source of healing

Nails as a means for release from pain

¬ T H E   H E A R T   O F   T H E   M A T T E R

Amongst the <u>GRIS-GRIS</u>, or fetishes, the chest has long been a psychological and aesthetic focus.
Because it is associated with the heart, the chest is often considered a source of life.
The Fon people use the expression ku hun, or 'dead heart'. It has a positive meaning in that
it conveys the qualities of patience, calmness and tranquillity.

These fetishes are often presented in large groupings, where the chest area of each figure is pierced
with nails or bound tightly with cord or other material. Although these fetishes
appear aggressive, they are used for healing purposes. In case of illness, the supplicant drives
a nail into the wood.

✤

<u>HE WILL BE HEALED</u>.

¬ E V I L   R E F L E C T E D

This gris-gris is made to both defend the owner and injure others who wish him harm. Inside the fetish are hair and nails from its owner. The body is covered with metal shards and bits of mirror. These two materials are responsible for sensing danger and turning it back. If the owner is cursed, the bad thoughts will be reflected back to the sender and destroy him.

¬ H E A L I N G   B O T T L E

Like the telephone, the healing bottle requires a generous splash of the owner's perfume to become activated. The bottle contains samples of the owner's <u>HAIR AND NAILS</u>,

Its other contents remain a mystery. The symbol of the <u>RED CROSS</u> is incorporated in this example because it is recognized all over the world to have a positive power. The bottle is seen as a talisman to bring good luck and protection to the traveler. Its small size make it easily portable.

¬ **M E S S A G E**

I N A B O T T L E

Assins, representing the owner's ancestors, are
employed as protection against enemies.
Anyone attempting to send a curse
to the bottle's owner risks death himself.

¬ THE FA DIVINING BOARD

The Bokounon has access to knowledge about each person's destiny because he can read the Fa.
In the system of the Fa, there are 256 signs (16 x 16). The particular destiny placed in each child's hands before birth
find its equivalent in one of these signs and this sign is retained until death.

The Bokounons have two ways to read the Fa. He either throws sixteen pieces of cola nut onto a surface
and interpret a supplicant's fate according to the configuration of the nuts, or,
alternately, he can use his own board. The believer's hand is guided to the white powder surface, made of crushed bone,
upon which he makes lines. Usually a panel of Boukonons debate for hours over the interpretation of the lines
before they advise the supplicant. It is a very complex process.

~~I PRINCE~~

THE POWER

GOUNON, MY FATHER HAD THE GIFT, THE CALLING. BUT HE THOUGHT OF HIMSELF AS A MODERN MAN, AND REFUSED TO BECOME ~~VOODES~~ VOODOOSI.

HE DIED WITHIN THREE WEEKS.

PRIESTS, PRIESTESSES, NOVICES, INITIATES

¬ M A H O U N O N A N D H I S S U C C E S S O R

Mahounon had a premonition that he would die before his time. HE CONSULTED THE FA, or oracle, to locate someone to succeed him as High Priest of the Mahoulissa monastery. Eventually, the Fa declared that Mahounon's successor was twelve years old, attended school, and was somewhere within fifty kilometers of the monastery.

A child was found who looked very promising. His father was known to have had the gift, the calling, but he had thought of himself as a modern man and refused to become a Voodoo priest. He died within three weeks. With the support of his grandfather, the child was kidnapped from his mother. The authorities take no action in such cases.

HE WAS GIVEN A NEW NAME: GOUNON, the god of iron. From this moment on, no one was allowed to use his old name. He now had a new family. Mahounon became Gounon's father, his wife, Gounon's mother.

THE POWER

¬ **N A L E**
Ten-year-old Na, Queen of the Mahoulissa monastery.

¬ AN   EMISSARY

An Achina Voodoosi at the investiture celebrations in Gounon's honor.

HIGH PRIEST MAHOUNON
deliberates over a suggestion from the council of the Mahoulissa monastery.

⌐ D A N , T H E R A I N B O W S N A K E

A Voodoo follower in front of the Temple of Dan, the Rainbow Snake. Like Mahoulissa,
Dan is both <u>MALE AND FEMALE</u>, the god of the air and the firmament.
He controls wealth, professional activity and continuity.
When he wishes to bestow wealth on a mortal, <u>HE TAKES ON HUMAN FORM</u>.

Clad as a beggar, he rewards the man who takes pity on him with gold and silver.

MAHINOU DÉHOUSSOU SANTOS, FROM QUARTIER LÉBOU OUIDAH

was born one of <u>TRIPLETS</u>. When the other two did not survive the birth,
Mahinou's mother consulted the Fa, and it was decided that her daughter would dedicate herself
to the Voodoo power of Déhoussou. Only women may take part in the ceremonies of worship,
which take place on the beach every Friday. So passionate is her devotion to Déhoussou,
that she has <u>LEFT HER CHILDREN</u> in the hands of her husband so that she has more time
to pray.

¬ S U P R E M E   C H I E F   O F
T H E   V O O D O O S I

Daagbo Hounon, Supreme Chief of the Voodoosi of Benin and official government representative of the Voodoo cult. He claims he came FROM THE OCEAN, and will return there when he dies. His staff is planted firmly in the power center before his throne.

THE POWER

K P A S S E N O N ,   K I N G   O F
O U I D A H   A N D   G U A R D I A N   O F
T H E   S A C R E D   F O R E S T ,

is the real Voodoo high priest in West Africa. No one is allowed to enter the Sacred Forest,
which is inhabited by the souls of the dead, without Kpassenon's permission.
His headdress **PROTECTS** others from the power of his gaze. It is said that if anyone looks
Kpassenon directly in the eyes, he will go blind.

¬ K P A S S E N O N
B E C O M E S   K I N G

Kpassenon used to be a Vespa mechanic. One night, two leopards appeared
to him in <u>A DREAM WITH A MESSAGE</u>: he was to be
the new king of the Sacred Forest. The next day, Kpassenon went to the current
king and guardian and told him of his dream. The king wanted proof,
so the two of them entered the Sacred Forest together. As they stood before a
huge tree, they were surprised b a wild storm. The tree was brought down
by the winds.

Two weeks later, on July 14, 1988, the two men returned to the same place in
the forest. Another storm passed. They had to lie down on the ground
to protect themselves. When the wind died down, the tree was standing again.

🐲

This was proof enough for the old king. <u>HE DECLARED KPASSENON THE
NEW KING AND GUARDIAN OF THE SACRED FOREST</u>.

¬ I N I T I A T E S

Kpassenon has his own initiates, who live in the forests. Their facial scarification represents the claws of a leopard. The initiates' responsibility is to <u>KEEP THE DEAD IN THE SACRED FOREST COMPANY</u>.

Kpassenon in his worldly hat.

Kpassenon was later to be elected to one of the highest positions in Benin's Voodoo hierarchy.

¬ **T H E   K I N G   O F   Y O R U B A**
on his throne in Ouidah. As with Kpassanon, his headdress <u>PREVENTS OTHERS FROM BEING BLINDED</u> when they look into his eyes. The throne next to him is reserved for his guests, who are directed to look at the opposite wall and not at the King.

¬ TRADITIONAL HEALER AND
MINISTER OF JUSTICE

Dako Wêgbé Nestor of Bohicon, traditional healer, Prime Minister and Minister of Justice
for Roi Dako, in his living room.

¬ K A H O U L A
Alpha Ousseni, <u>TRADITIONAL HEALER</u>
from Parakou with his kahoula, the fetish
which predicts the safety and success
of travelers. His second specialty is diabetes.

¬ G U A R D I A N   O F   T H E   L E G B A

Legbanon Gandoto Fandi, Guardian of the Agadje Legba in Quartier Fonssalamé.
This is the most important Legba in Benin. Centuries ago, <u>ENSLAVED CHILDREN WERE BURIED ALIVE</u>
inside the Legba. This is the source of its tremendous power.

¬ THE SORCERESS
ZANGBAN

The Sorceress Zangban is eighty-five years old and nearly blind. She lives alone because she is so feared by the community. Before she dies, she will hand her power on to another woman.

The woman will have no choice in this: <u>THE POWER IS HERS UNTIL SHE DIES.</u>

AMAZONS

The Linsouhoulé are the <u>REINCARNATION OF THE AMAZONS</u> of the past,
the all-female cavalry, who were once the fiercest fighters in the king's army.
The prisoners of war captured by these Amazons were later sold as slaves to European traders.
The uniform of the Amazons carries the <u>SYMBOL OF THE KING</u> and includes a
dagger and a saber. While in uniform, they may not leave the monastery, nor be touched.

They have no scarification, live only part-time in the monastery,
and are allowed to marry. However, within the walls of the monastery there is
<u>NO CONTACT BETWEEN MEN AND WOMEN.</u>

The husband of an Amazon, or Linsouhoulé.

¬ T H E   R E C O N C I L I A T I O N

One day Mahoulissa, the Supreme God and ruler of the heavens descended to earth in the guise
of a woman guided by two leopards. She came upon a king with no crown wandering with his
subjects in the desert.

She asked him why they were not home, in their kingdom. The king replied that they'd suffered a famine
and were searching for food. No matter what they did to HONOR THE GODS OF VOODOO,
it was never right. Legba accepted their offerings, but punished them with drought or plague or worse.
He took their women and stole their money.

Mahouulissa asked: "And still, you honor the gods of voodoo?"

The king replied yes.

Mahoulissa began to weep at the wrong her mischievous son had done. And as her tears
turned the rocks and dust into rich plants and fertile fields, the king and his subjects understood
who the woman really was.

"I will send you three prophets," said Mahoulissa, "and they will teach you to read the Fa,
the oracle which determines your destiny. Then you will know yourself what to do to please the gods,
and my son will no longer be able to harm you.

This is the key to your freedom. And this you must pass on from generation to generation.
Until the end of the world."

THE KING

Agoli Agbo, King of Abomey

There are two kings in Abomey at present. They are no rivals, but have their own followers.
Sa majesté le roy Houedognie Gbehanzhin, Roy de Benin, surrounded by princesses and wifes in his
throne room in Abomey.

King Agoli Agbo with some of his forty-two wives. He has to wear a <u>SILVER SIEVE</u> over his
nose at all times so he doesn't breathe the same air as normal people.
He's not allowed to leave the royal compound, and visitors must speak to him through
his foreign minister, never directly. He must eat alone and it is forbidden for him to see the ocean.
Before his coronation he used to work as a policeman in Porto Novo.

TIGHT

THE ROAD TO TRANCE

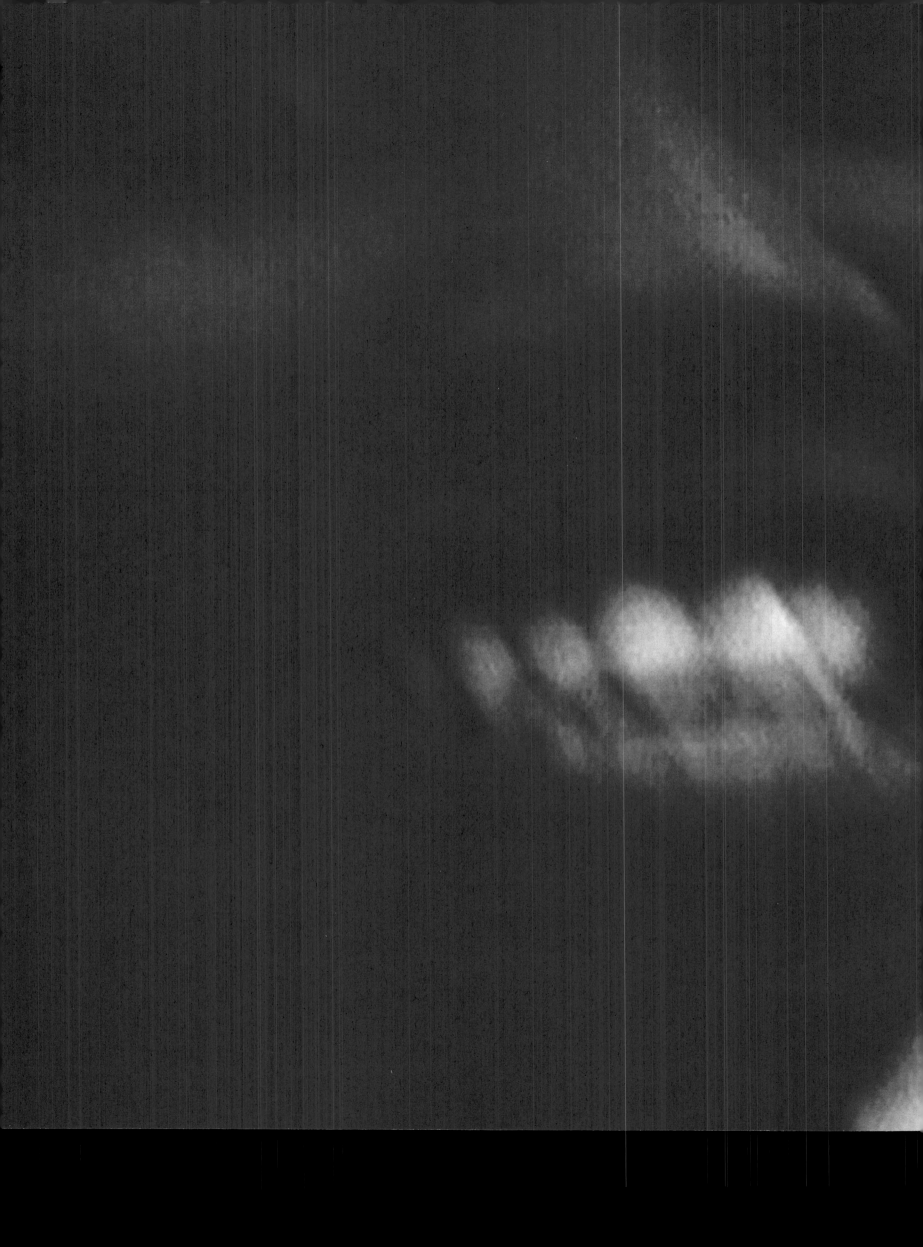

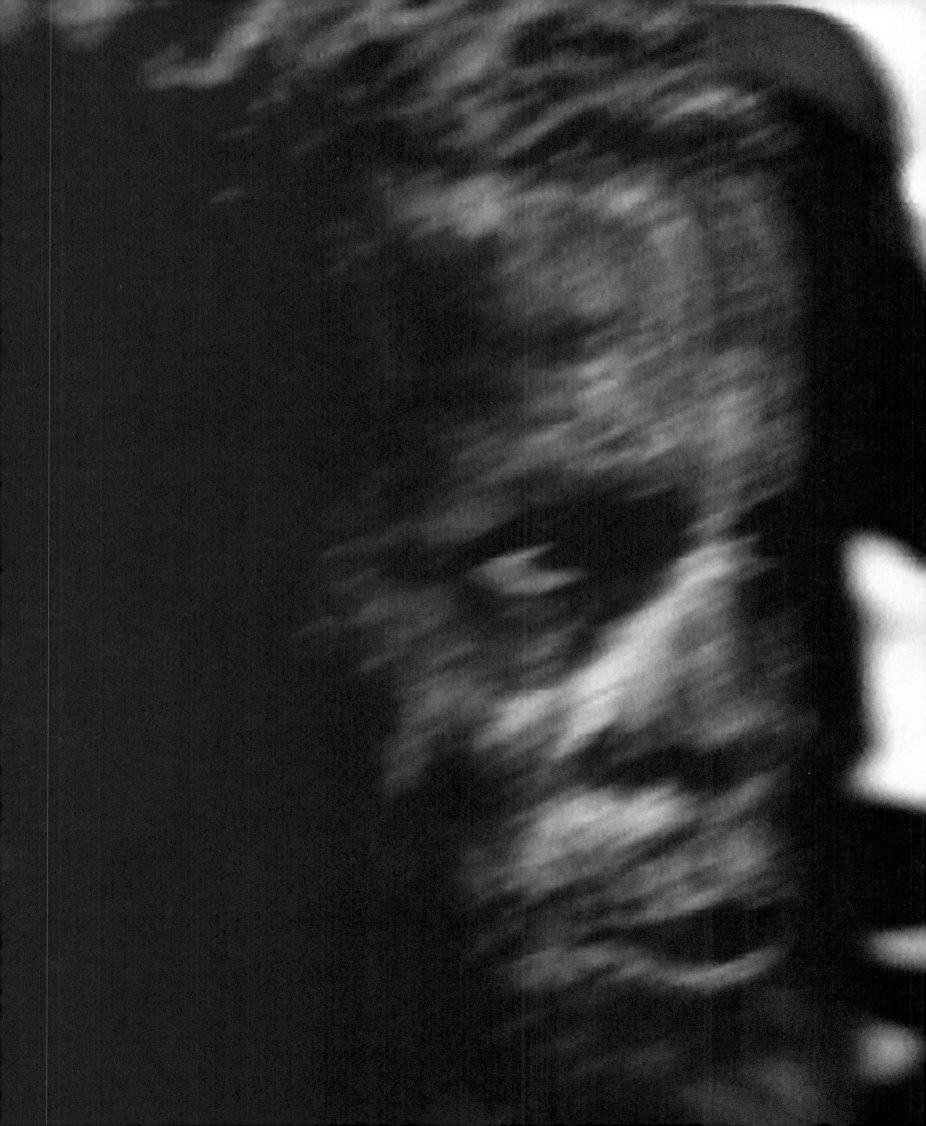

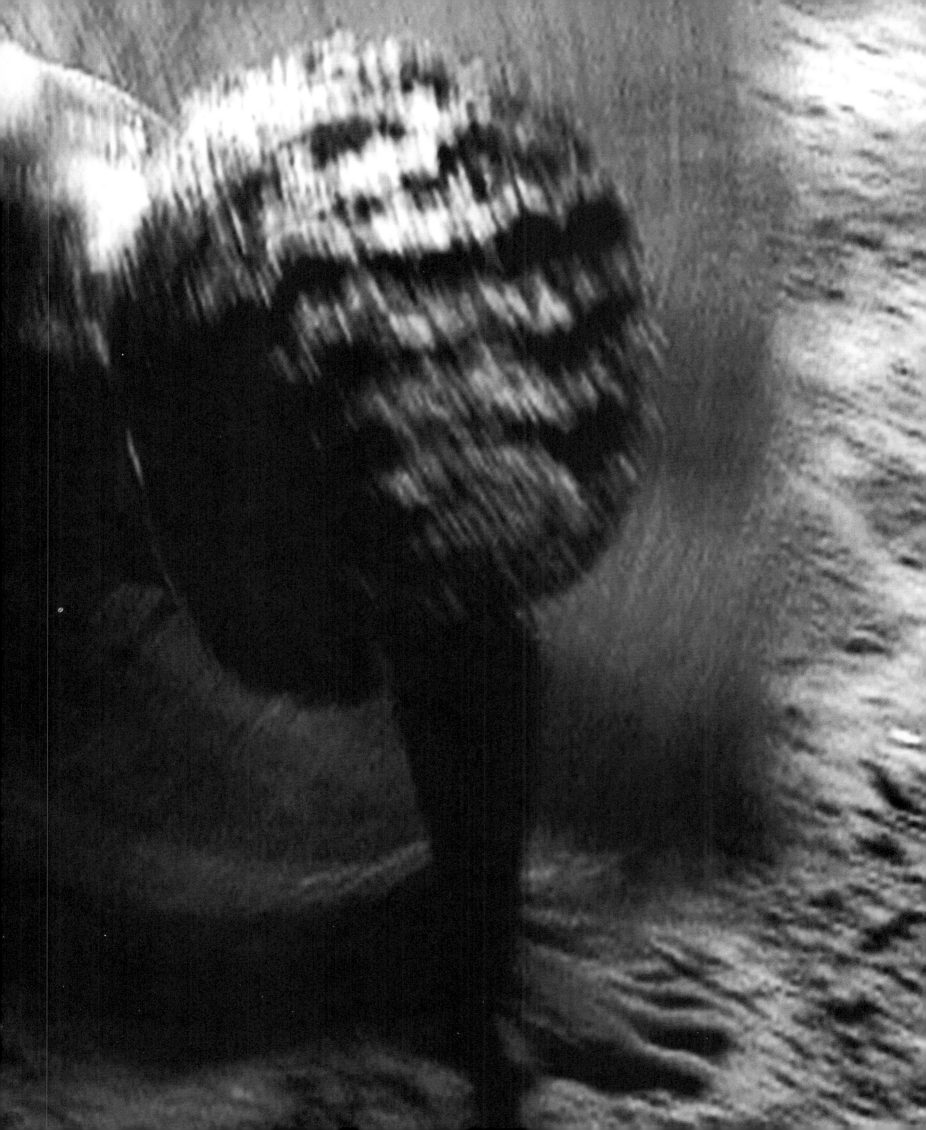

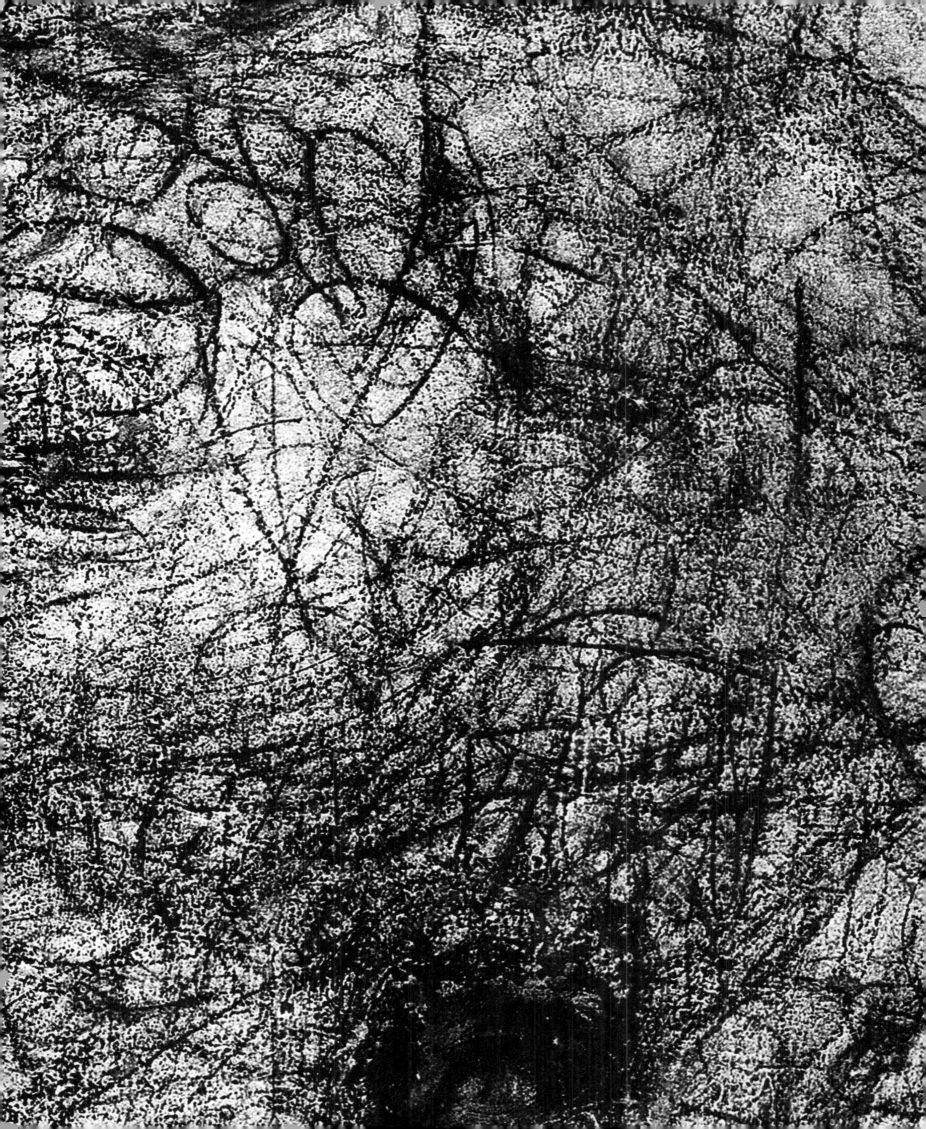

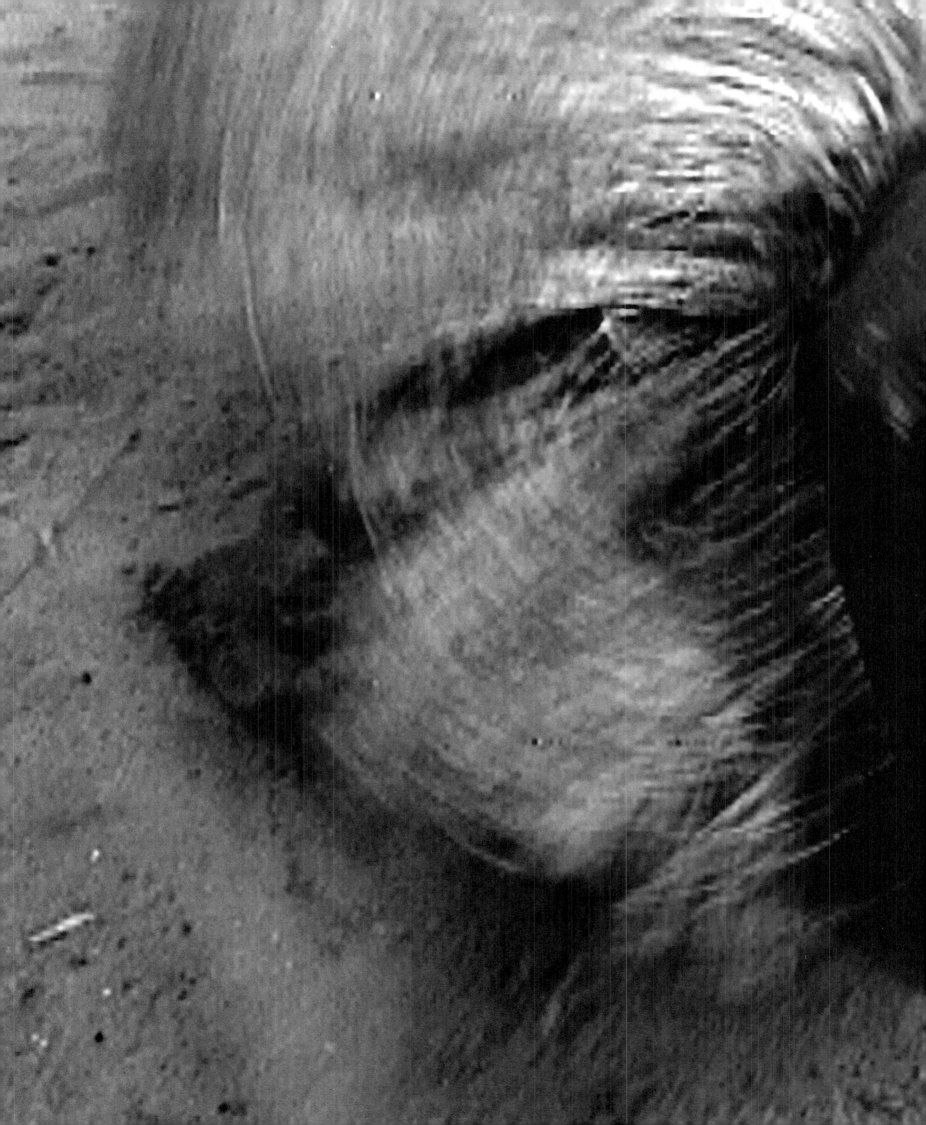

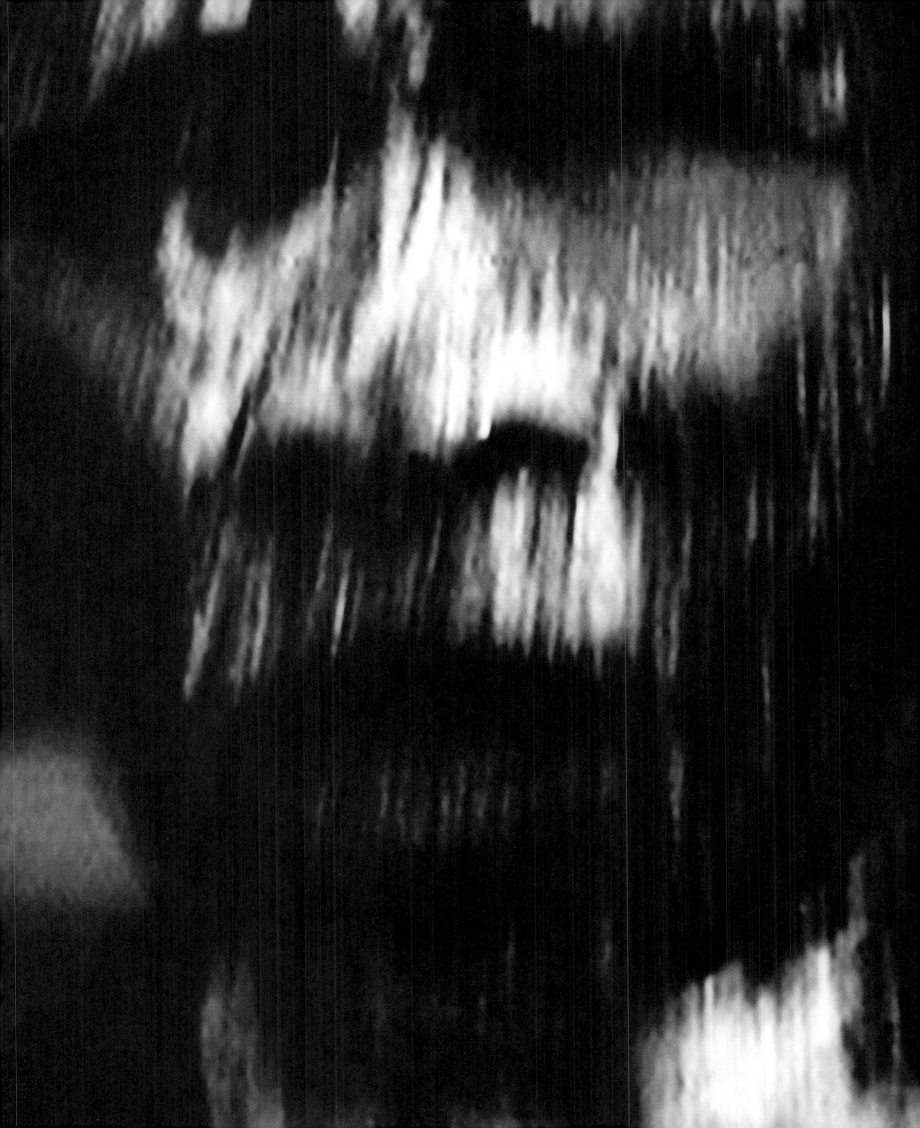

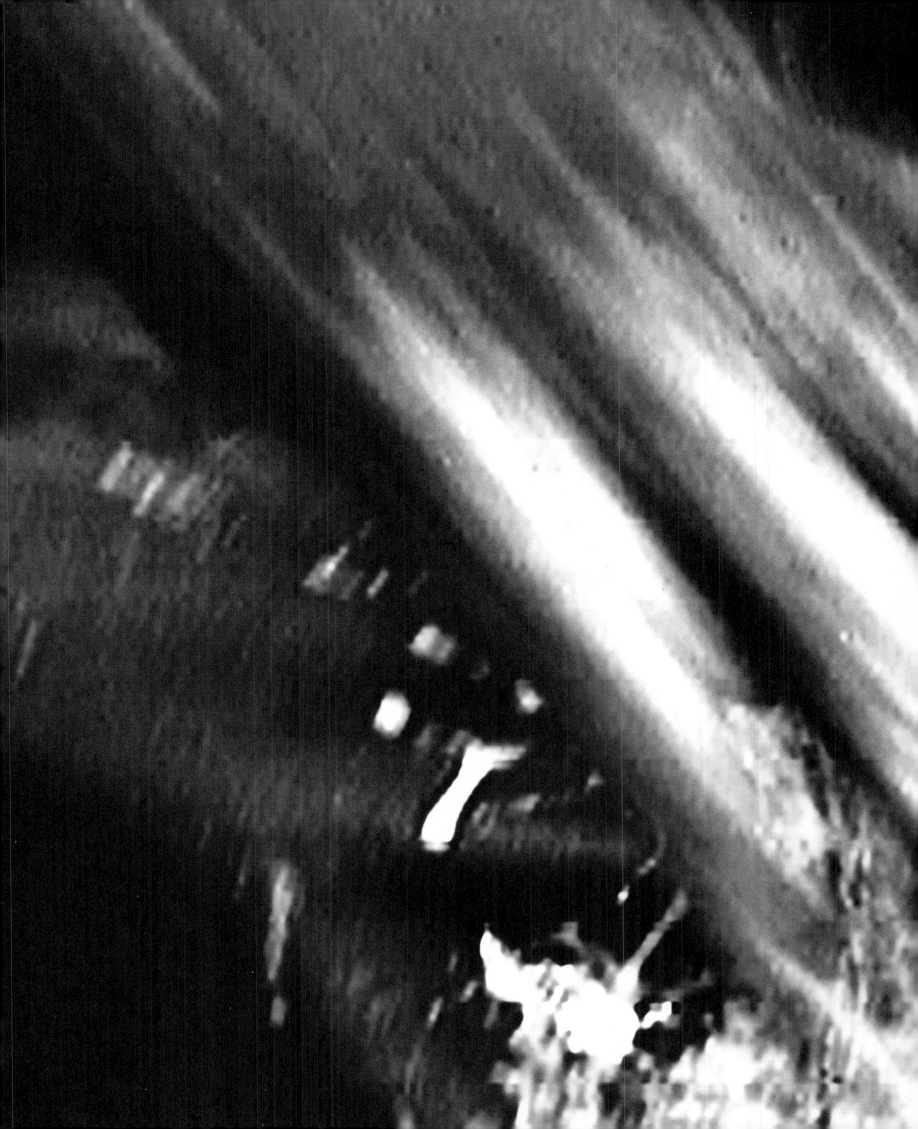

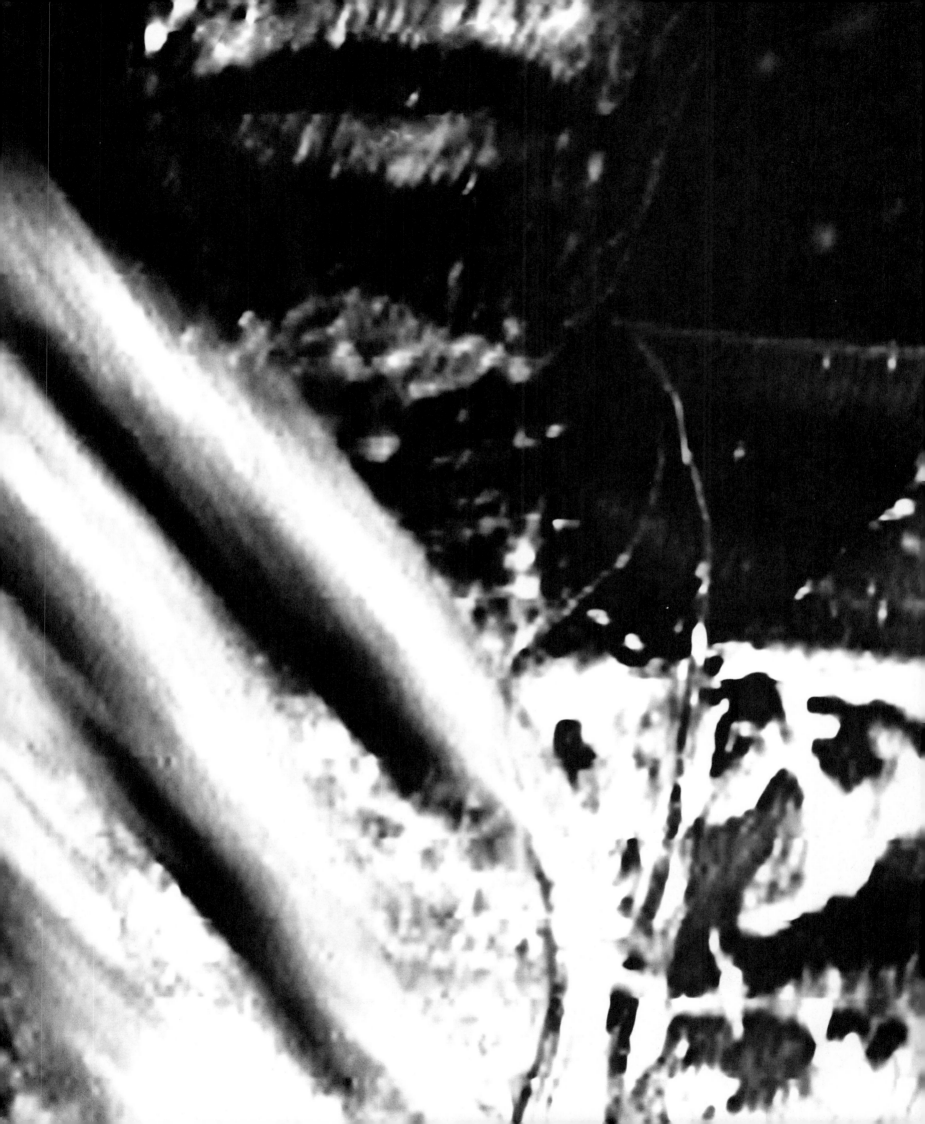

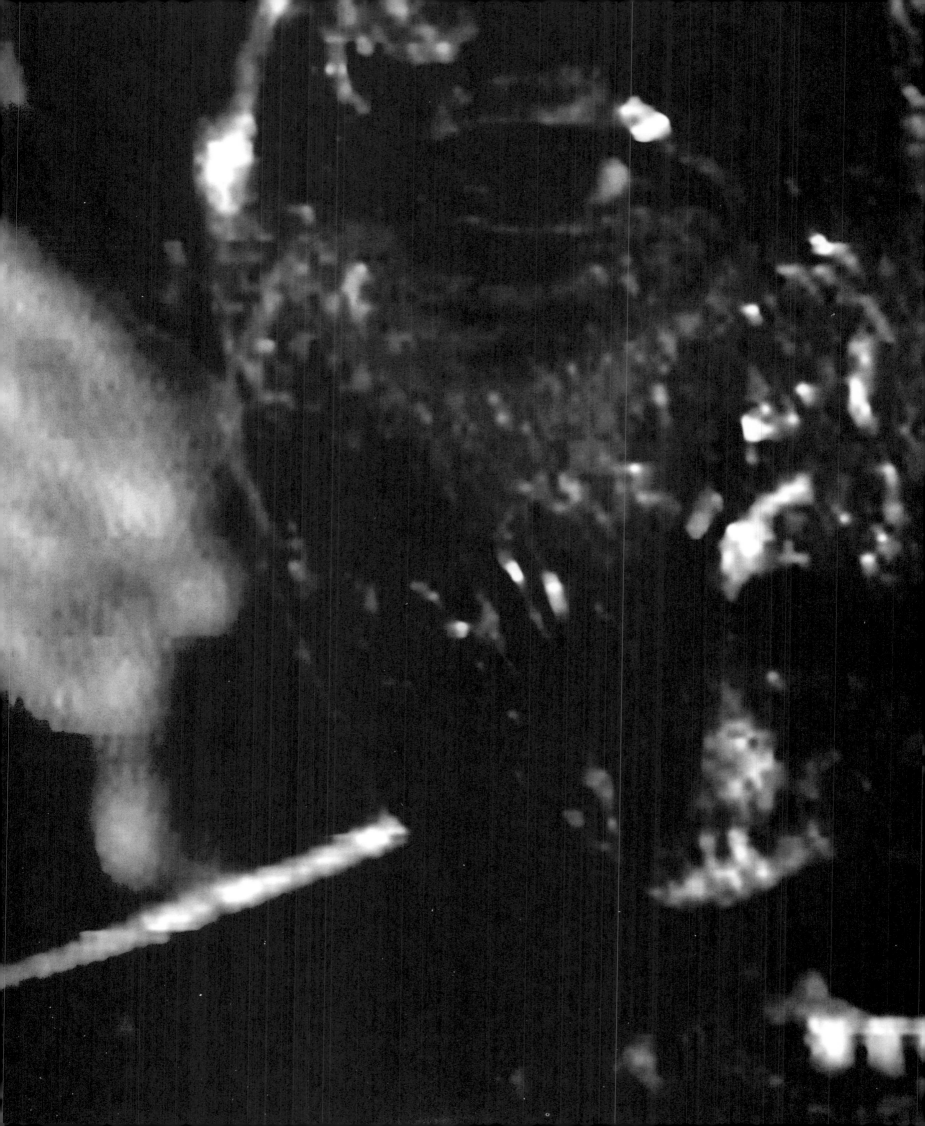

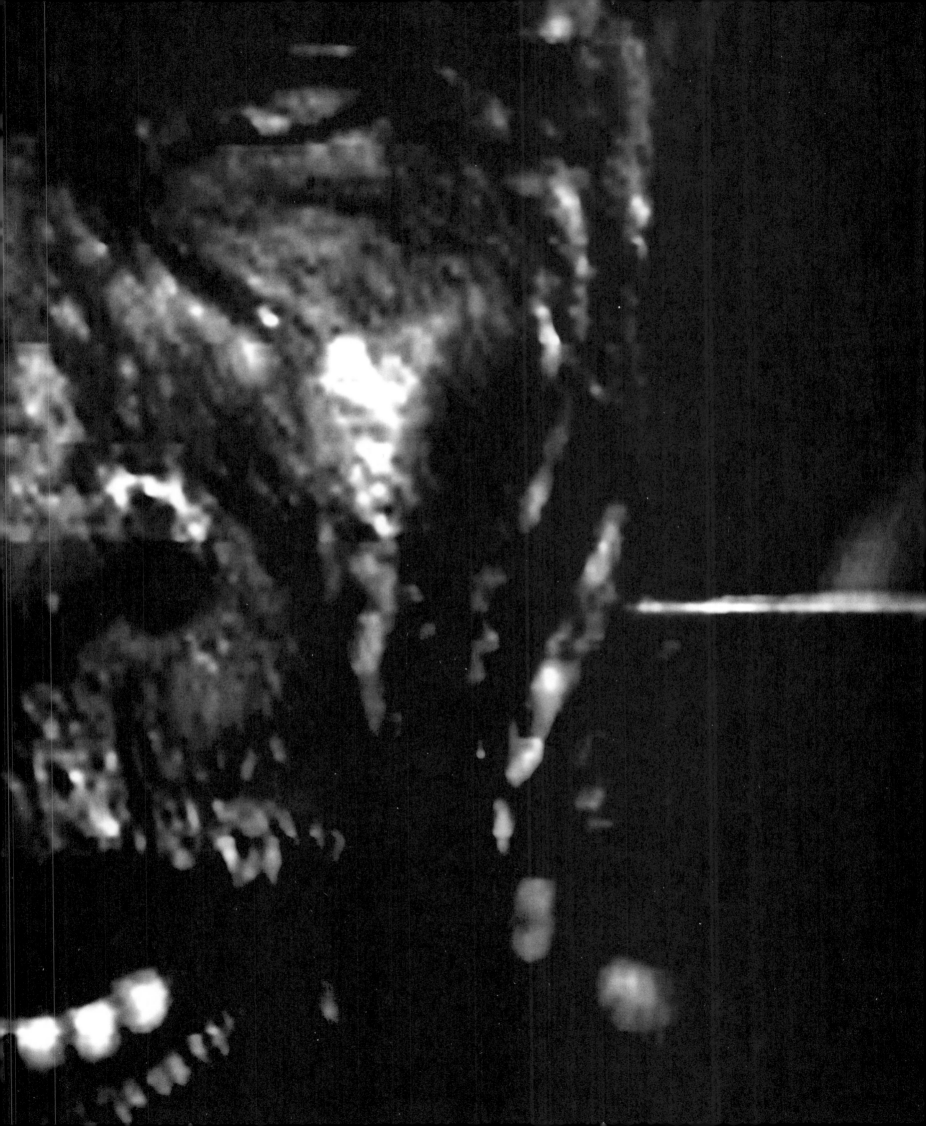

27

VORWORT VON WIM WENDERS

¬SCHWARZWEIßE MAGIE Als Alberto Venzago mir seinen (damals noch unfertigen) Film Mounted by the Gods zum ersten Mal zeigte, nannte ich ihn spontan den »Film eines Fotografen«, war mir aber nicht so sicher, ob er das als Auszeichnung verstehen wollte (als solche war es zweifellos gemeint, denn fotografisch ist der Film ein regelrechtes Wunderwerk). Als ich dann aber den hier vorliegenden Fotoband umgekehrt gar als »Buch eines Filmemachers« bezeichnete, hatte ich es mir mit Alberto wahrscheinlich erst einmal verdorben. Vielleicht gelingt es mir im Folgenden, ihm beides nicht als paradox, sondern als Komplimente schmackhaft zu machen...

Fotografie, ob man will oder nicht, hat ja immer etwas ›Punktuelles‹, beleuchtet den jeweiligen Moment, hält eben einen ganz bestimmten Augenblick fest. Auch Bilder aus der Welt der Voodoo-Religion, so darf man zu Recht annehmen, stellen solche Momentaufnahmen dar. Zumindest erwartet man genau das von einem Magnum-Fotografen. Beim Durchblättern dieses Buches und beim Eintauchen in sein außergewöhnliches Universum, wie es sich da langsam aus dem Schwarz herausschält, stellt sich aber etwas ganz anderes ein: ein deutliches Gefühl von Dauer! In der Abfolge dieser Bilder entsteht eine andere Summe als die von Fotografien gewohnte: nämlich ZEIT!

Eigentlich ist es ja nur das Erzählen, das diese Dimension herstellt, also das Einbringen einer Fiktion. Aber erzählt Venzago uns in den Bildern dieses Buches eine Geschichte? Sind Buch und Film nicht ›Dokumente‹? Oder doch Erfindungen? Kann man beim Betrachten des Films und des Buches ›seinen Augen trauen‹? Vielleicht muß man ein bisschen von der Herstellungsgeschichte des Films und dieser Fotografien wissen, um im wahrsten Sinne des Wortes Licht ins Dunkel zu bringen.

Vor fünfzehn Jahren, im April 1988 genau, will Venzago mit einer Vespa den afrikanischen Kontinent durchqueren. Er fotografiert im Auftrag von GEO. Die Pisten sind schlaglochübersät und versinken in Regenfluten. Die Pannen häufen sich. Schließlich gibt die Vespa in der Stadt Ouidah in Benin endgültig ihren Geist auf. Alberto fotografiert die mit Graffiti bemalte Mauer, vor der er stehen geblieben ist. Er weiß noch nicht, dass hinter der Mauer ein berühmtes Voodoo-Kloster liegt und dass der freundliche dicke Mann im wallenden Gewand, der dem gestrandeten Fotografen seine Hilfe anbietet, Mahounon selbst ist, der diesem Kloster vorsteht, einer der einflussreichsten Voodoo-Priester Westafrikas. Mit dem Orakel, das Mahounon dem Schweizer wenig später liest, beginnt dessen Faszination für Voodoo: Was er da aus seiner eigenen Vergangenheit und aus seinem eigenen Leben zu hören bekommt, kann dieser Priester nach menschlichem Ermessen unmöglich gewusst haben...

Die beiden ungleichen Männer freunden sich an. Es entsteht ein Vertrauensverhältnis, das es Venzago erlaubt, zwei Jahre später mit Dreharbeiten zu beginnen, die sich über zwölf Jahre erstrecken sollten. In dieser Zeit kehrt er wieder und wieder nach Benin zurück und darf Zeremonien und Rituale filmen, die vor ihm noch niemand aufzeichnen konnte und die wohl nie wieder jemand so unverstellt zu Gesicht bekommen wird. Alberto ist dieser Film sozusagen ›auf den letzten Drücker‹ gelungen, im letzten Moment der Unschuld auch dieses Teils der Welt.

Eine erstaunliche Geschichte tut sich vor ihm auf: Mahounon ahnt seinen Tod voraus, eigentlich weit vor der Zeit – noch ist er in den besten Jahren. Aber er drängt darauf, rechtzeitig einen Nachfolger zu finden, um ihn in die Geheimnisse seines Amtes einzuweihen. Kinder aus dem ganzen Land werden in das Kloster gebracht, aber nach dem einjährigen, höchst anstrengenden Noviziat wird keines von ihnen vom Fa, dem Orakel des Voodoo, angenommen. Stattdessen weisen alle Zeichen auf einen 12-jährigen Jungen aus dem Nachbarort: Gounon.

Seine Mutter will ihren Sohn nicht ins Kloster ziehen lassen, so wird er gegen ihren Willen entführt. Venzago filmt, wie Gounon vier Jahre lang ausgebildet und in die Geheimnisse seiner Religion eingeführt wird. Der Junge erfährt von seinem Lehrer alles, was ein Hohepriester kennen muß: schwarze und weiße Magie, ekstatische Tänze und das rätselhafte Wirken des Orakels.

Mahounon stirbt in der Tat vorzeitig und plötzlich. Alberto ist mit seiner Kamera dabei, als Gounon vor der Wahl steht, letztlich zu jung und unvorbereitet in die Fußstapfen seines Meisters zu treten. Aber nach schweren Prüfungen wird er als 17-Jähriger von allen mächtigen Voodoo-Größen des Landes anerkannt. Der König des Landes selbst nimmt ihn in einer feierlichen Zeremonie in den Kreis der Hohepriester auf...

Je mehr man vom Sog dieser Geschichte ergriffen wird, umso mehr will man sie als Fiktion begreifen. Zu märchenhaft erscheint einem diese Welt, zu unwahrscheinlich heutzutage, von unserer Warte aus gesehen. Im Film sowie im Buch enthält sich Venzago aller Deutung. Er gibt keine ethnologischen Erklärungen an die Hand, zeigt nur alles, was er sieht, ganz phänomenologisch. Aber er lässt die Bilder trotzdem nicht auf sich allein gestellt: Er stellt ihnen einige Fabeln und Mythen aus der Welt des Voodoo zur Seite, vorgetragen von einem machtvollen Erzähler, dessen Stimme den Zuschauer in ihren Bann zieht.

Man erfährt so geradezu beiläufig auch das Notwendigste, um der Geschichte von Mahounon und Gounon folgen zu können, aber es sind vor allem diese Wesen aus einer fremdartigen, unerhörten Schöpfungsgeschichte, die es einem erlauben, einen Blick hinter den Schleier dieser Religion zu werfen.

Auch das Buch enthält diese Erzählungen, die hier ganz anders wirken als im Film. Dabei ist es Venzago gelungen, aus dem Durchblättern dieser Bilder und dem Lesen der Texte ein geradezu filmisches Erlebnis zu machen. Es entsteht dabei so etwas wie ein Rhythmus, der das Papier in Bewegung geraten und den Eindruck entstehen lässt, als begännen diese Schwarzweiß-Fotos wirklich zu tanzen und die Trance-Zustände, die in ihnen eingefangen sind, lebendiger und wirklicher zu erscheinen, als man von Fotobüchern gewohnt ist. (Im Film ist ihm da etwas ähnlich Magisches gelungen: Da kommt die Farbe nämlich aus dieser schwarzweißen Welt heraus und verschwindet dann wieder, ohne dass man die Übergänge bemerkt hätte.)

Um beim Anschauen des Buches aber ähnlich selbstvergessen davontragen zu lassen, wie es dem Film gelingt, empfehle ich, dazu den Soundtrack aufzulegen und möglichst laut zu stellen. Venzago und seine Musiker, Boris Blank, Peter Scherer und Jochen Schmidt-Hambrock, haben da etwas Kühnes gewagt: Basierend auf realen Tonaufnahmen von Tänzen und Zeremonien lassen sie eine neue zeitgenössische Musik entstehen, aus Samples und Loops aufgebaut, die allen Flair und den Wirbel der Originalmusiken beinhaltet. Diese wird aber gleichzeitig ›übersetzt‹, um sie uns näher zu bringen und mehr unter die Haut gehen zu lassen, als es der ethnologisch korrekte Sound wohl könnte.

Genau das tut diese Arbeit, dieses Gesamtwerk aus Bildern und Tönen: Es geht einem unter die Haut! Was man da gesehen und gehört hat, kann man anschließend nicht einfach abstreifen. Zu vieles daran ist unerklärlich, nicht bloß die Mischung aus Fiktion und Wahrheit, aus Vorgegaukeltem und Tatsächlichem, aus dem aufblasbaren Air France Jumbo und den todmüden Kinderaugen.

Was das für ein Film ist und was für ein Buch, kann ich, je besser ich beide kenne, immer weniger sagen. Insofern nehme ich meine ersten Definitionen zurück, wahrscheinlich zu deiner Erleichterung, Alberto. Aber eines weiß ich mit Bestimmtheit: Was du da aus zwölf Jahren der erstaunlichsten Erfahrungen und aus über hundert Stunden Videomaterial und Tausenden von Negativen herausdestilliert hast, das hat es noch nicht gegeben, weder im Kino noch in der Fotografie, das ist einmalig im wahrsten Sinne des Wortes.

35
ALBERTO VENZAGO

¬PRIVATE OBSESSION, PUBLIC AFFAIR Allada, Abéokouta, Afagnagan: Namen wie Steine an einer Schnur. Eine Perlenkette voller Städte, jeder Stein ein Dorf. Dassa, Savinou, Kilkibo, Parakou, Ouidah: Namen von Kleinstaaten und Königreichen. Träume von Menschen. Auch meine eigenen.

Es ist Frühling 1988. Diesmal sollte meine Reise kein Ziel haben. Ich wollte das andere Afrika erfahren, das Afrika meiner Kindheit. Ich rieche noch die vergilbten Seiten alter Bildbände über die Entdecker, die schwarzweißen Stiche von riesigen Urwäldern, nie gesehenen Tieren, gewaltigen Stromschnellen und kirchturmhohen Wasserfällen. Ich wollte diese Erregung wieder spüren. Ich wollte eintauchen in ein unbegreifliches Leben.

Nach jahrelangen Reportagen über die Unterdrückten und die Mächtigen hatte ich Afrika bislang vor allem als Spezialist für das Grässliche kennen gelernt. Meine Bilder aus jener Zeit zeigen ausgemergelte Körper in Hungersnöten, finster dreinblickende Despoten nach dem neuesten Militärputsch oder Motive im Schleier einer verklärten Romantik des ›homme sauvage‹. Ich machte mich mit einer Vespa auf den Weg. Ohne Ziel. Ohne Zeitlimit. Einfach quer durch Afrika. Auf der Suche nach etwas Unbekanntem.

Ich fand, was ich suchte, als ich gezwungen wurde, zu verweilen. Ein Motorschaden setzte mich in Ouidah fest, einer kleinen Stadt in Benin/Westafrika. So kam es, dass ich Mahounon begegnete, einem der höchsten Voodoo-Priester Afrikas – für mich der Beginn einer langen geistigen Reise.

Natürlich war das für mich damals Zufall. Schließlich hätte auch in Togo oder Ghana oder sonst irgendwo auf meiner Reise etwas Außergewöhnliches passieren können. Dachte ich damals.

Benin – früher einmal das Königreich von Dahomey – war ein schwarzes Sparta, eingeklemmt zwischen den Völkern der Yoruba im heutigen Nigeria und den Ewe in Ostghana und Togo. Der Legende nach geht das Königsgeschlecht von Dahomey auf eine Prinzessin aus Adja und einen Leoparden zurück, der sie am Ufer des Mono verführte. Ihre Könige schmückten sich seither mit Klauenabdrücken an ihren Schläfen.

Die gefürchtetsten Krieger Dahomeys waren Frauen, und ihre einzige nennenswerte Einkommensquelle die Versklavung und der Verkauf unterjochter Nachbarvölker. Nach dem Tod eines Königs zog sein Nachfolger traditionell in den Krieg, um neue Stämme zu unterwerfen. Denn es war seine Pflicht, den Reichtum des Landes zu vergrößern.

In diesem von Kriegen und Raubzügen heimgesuchten Landstrich, der später als Sklavenküste traurige Berühmtheit erlangen sollte, entstand der Voodoo-Kult. Und mit den Sklaven wurde er in die ganze Welt exportiert. Nach dem Ende der Sklaverei versank Benin in Vergessenheit. Von der Natur ohne nennenswerte Bodenschätze wie Erdöl oder Diamanten ausgestattet und neben seinen weitaus größeren Nachbarn geopolitisch bedeutungslos, rückte das Land an die Peripherie, an der der Fortschritt für lange Zeit fast spurlos vorüberging. So konnte sich ein sehr ursprüngliches Leben erhalten.

Obwohl von Missionaren aller Religionen und Politikern jeder Couleur bekämpft, blieb Voodoo immer ein fester Bestandteil der Gesellschaft. 35 Prozent der Einwohner Benins sind Christen, 25 Prozent Muslime. Gleichzeitig gehören 80 Prozent dem Voodoo-Glauben an. Und

diese Statistik ist weniger das Ergebnis einer verunglückten Volkszählung als vielmehr der bewundernswerten Toleranz der Afrikaner gegenüber Religionen.

Mit Hilfe Mahounons tauchte ich in eine andere Welt ein: Er erklärte mir das Klosterleben und ließ mich an gut gehüteten Zeremonien teilhaben. Vor allem aber faszinierte mich die unschuldige Natürlichkeit der Menschen. Seither verbringe ich jedes Jahr einige Monate hier.

Ohne jeglichen anthropologischen Hintergrund hatte ich mich auf eine Reise ins Unbekannte begeben. Ich wollte lieber die Orientierung verlieren, als nach vordergründigen Antworten suchen. »Selbst viele Worte füllen keinen Korb«, sagt ein Sprichwort aus Ghana.

Ich fühle mich wohl bei diesen Menschen. Jeder Besuch öffnet mehr Türen. Das Unbekannte wird bekannter, doch je länger ich da bin, je mehr ich die Rituale zu kennen meine, desto mehr lassen mich die Voodoosi spüren, dass ich noch nichts weiß. Vertrauen wird einem nicht geschenkt, es muss erarbeitet werden.

Fast unbemerkt spannte sich über die Jahre ein Bogen zwischen meinen beiden großen Leidenschaften: der Fotografie und der Beschäftigung mit Ritualen. Dabei wollte ich versuchen, nicht zu vereinfachen und keine Allgemeinplätze, Klischees, Halbwahrheiten zu bestätigen.

Eines Tages erklärte mir Mahounon, dass nicht ich nach Afrika gekommen sei, um ein Abenteuer zu erleben, sondern dass er mich geholt habe, um seine Geschichte zu dokumentieren. Wie auch immer – das Ergebnis sind zwölf Jahre Arbeit. Daraus entstanden ein Film, eine CD und dieses Buch.

Es ist Hochsommer, als ich an den Beerdigungszeremonien Mahounons teilnehme. In der Grabkammer ist es stockdunkel. Während ich das spärliche Licht messe, beginnen die Oberpriester mit der Zeremonie. Rückwärts, in halbgebückter Stellung bewegen sie sich unter Trommelschlägen langsam mit einer Ziege und einem Huhn in die Grabkammer, während die Klostergemeinde draußen in der brütenden Hitze tanzt und singt. Ich möchte gerade anfangen zu filmen, da überreichen mir Kpassenon und die Priester des Mahou Lissa-Kultes einen Fetisch. Über neun Jahre lang bin ich immer Journalist geblieben. Den schmalen Grat vom Beobachter zum Teilnehmer habe ich nie überschritten. Und außer Pierre Verger ist kein Weißer je ein Fatumbie geworden – ein Voodoopriester, ein Eingeweihter, ein Wissender. Jetzt bin ich ein Teil der Zeremonie. Das Filmen wird zur Nebensache.

Mahounons Prophezeiung hat sich erfüllt: Gounon wurde als sein Nachfolger inthronisiert. Handys und Farbfernsehen haben Einzug gehalten in diese unberührte Welt. Ouidah hat sich rasant verändert. Und auch seine Einwohner. Doch die Freundschaft ist mit dem Abschluss des Films und des Buches nicht abgebrochen. Sie bleibt bestehen.

Dieses Buch ist kein Fachbuch, es ist eine Einladung zu einer Reise. Eine Reise zu den Ursprüngen des Voodoo, zu Kpassenon, dem Hüter des heiligen Hains, und Aboli Ahgbo, dem König in Abomey mit seinen 42 Frauen. Zum Magier Fofo, der unliebsame Nebenbuhler telepathisch mit einer Dauererektion bestraft, zu Gounon, der mit seinen einundzwanzig Jahren die Last einer ganzen Klostergemeinschaft tragen muss. Zu einer Landschaft, die noch unberührt vom Touristenstrom ist. Zu Menschen, die von tiefer Gläubigkeit sind.

Mein Dank geht an alle Freunde in Ouidah, besonders an meinen Aufnahmeleiter Lambert Abagadan, der mir ein Afrika gezeigt hat, das mehr ist als ein Bild aus Kindertagen. Der Künstler Yves Pede, die Übersetzerin Martine de Souza, mein Freund und Voodoosi Gounon Tokpo, Kpassenon, der Hüter des heiligen Hains, der mich »mon prince« nennt, Fofo und die ganze Familie von Mahounon. Sie alle haben einen Platz in meinem Herzen.

Ein besonderer Dank geht an Thilo Röscheisen, der mich nicht nur großzügig mit Ideen und Texten bei diesem

Projekt unterstützt hat, sondern mir auch als Freund immer mit Rat und Tat zur Seite stand. Ich danke Kit Hopkins für ihre jahrelange Unterstützung und Inspiration seit dem Beginn meiner Obsession. Aus Legenden und Erzählungen, die ich wie ein Jäger und Sammler notierte, entstanden ihre wunderbaren Texte in Film und Buch.

Ich habe nicht nur in Afrika Freunde gewonnen. Wim und Donata Wenders sind in mein Leben getreten. Ich bin dankbar und froh, dass es sie gibt. Als ausführender Produzent hat Wim das Projekt unterstützt und mir Vertrauen in die Kraft der Bilder geschenkt.

Das Buch ist fertig. 125 Fotografien, im Schnitt mit 1/125 Sekunde fotografiert. Das ergibt total eine Sekunde. Eine Sekunde in Ouidah: a slice of time. Aber was bedeutet schon Zeit in Afrika. »Il y a trois jours«, hat Mahounon immer gesagt, auch wenn wir uns ein ganzes Jahr lang nicht gesehen hatten.

DIE DUNKELHEIT
PEOPLESCAPE

44
¬DIE ABIKOU VON DJOHITIN Hat eine Frau eine Fehlgeburt, fragt sie die Abikou um Rat. Sie macht ihnen ein Bündel Stoff zum Geschenk. Wenn sie dann wieder schwanger wird und ein gesundes Kind zur Welt bringt, zeigt sie das Neugeborene den Abikou. Diese ritzen ihm ein Zeichen auf die Wange. Ab diesem Zeitpunkt muss ihnen die Mutter jedes Jahr Geld, Essen – sogar eine ganze Ziege – bringen. Tut sie es nicht, wird sie Probleme haben. Die Abikou gelten als sehr gefährlich. Die Leute im Dorf haben Angst, von ihnen angesprochen zu werden: »So helft mir! Meine Kleider sind alt und schmutzig. Helft mir!« So betteln sie. Die Abikou haben hohe Stimmen und sprechen entweder Fon oder Yoruba. Sie dürfen nur untertags aus dem Haus und haben kein Anrecht auf die Nacht.

46
DIE ACHINA-HÜTER besuchen Mahounons Mahoulissa-Kloster und warten, um Gounon ihre Aufwartung zu machen. (Achina – links im Hintergrund – ist der ›Gral‹ des Voodoo.)

50
¬DIE SCHÖPFUNG Es war einmal eine Zeit voller Chaos und Finsternis. Feuersbrünste zerstörten unsere Wälder, die Ozeane tosten, und vom Himmel fiel kein Tropfen Regen mehr. Frauen gebaren Ziegen, keine Kinder. Wasserquellen versiegten, und die Erde war hart wie Stein. Es gab keine Ernte. Mütter verzweifelten am Hungertod ihrer Kinder. Es kam zum Streit in unserem Volk. Irgendjemand musste ja für das Unheil verantwortlich sein. Die Ältesten berieten verzweifelt, was zu tun sei. Doch sie wussten keine Lösung. Und das Leiden ging weiter. Eines Tages erschien eine Greisin aus dem Lande Adja. Sie war eine weise Frau, begleitet von zwei Leoparden. Sie sah auf unser Land voll Grauen und Finsternis und sprach zu unserem König: »Euer Leid wird erst enden, wenn ihr denen huldigt, die auch wir verehren, den Göttern des Voodoo.«

MAHOULISSA Die Mann-Frau Mahoulissa, höchste Göttin und Herrscher/in des Himmels, ist ein Wesen mit zwei Gesichtern. Das erste ist weiblich, und ihre Augen sind der Mond. Das andere ist männlich, und seine Augen sind die Sonne. Mahou beherrscht die Nacht und Lissa den Tag.

Da Mahoulissa sowohl Mann als auch Weib ist, wurde sie schwanger. Sie teilte das Universum unter ihren vielen Kindern auf: Die Erde ging an den Ältesten, die Himmel an die Zwillinge, die Meere an ihr Drittgeborenes und so weiter.

Doch für ihr jüngstes Kind, ihren verwöhnten Lieblingssohn Legba, war nichts mehr übrig. So machte Mahoulissa ihn zu ihrem Boten. Nur Legba kann mit allem Leben kommunizieren, sei es himmlisch oder weltlich. Er kann sehr boshaft und grausam sein. Der Schlüssel zu Legbas Wohlwollen sind Opfer – Blutopfer.

57
¬LEGBASSI Aufgabe dieser jungen Voodoo-Anhängerin ist es, während der dreitägigen Legbassi-Feiern das Publikum zu unterhalten. Im Mund hat sie Kolanüsse, die sie in 16 Stücke zerbeißt. Sie werden für das Fa-Orakel benötigt.

58/60
DIE HÖLZERNEN PUPPEN stellen Zwillinge oder Geschwister von Zwillingen einer Voodoo-Anhängerin dar, die – meist bei der Geburt – gestorben sind. Die Mutter oder Geschwister führen dann die Puppe (oder mehrere) Tag und Nacht mit sich: Das verstorbene Geschwisterteil lebt in ihr fort. Mutter oder Kind wissen, dass etwas Schreckliches passieren wird, wenn sie die Puppe vergessen oder verlieren. Die Puppe macht all das, was sie selbst auch tun. Ist die Zeit für eine Initiationsfeier gekommen, trägt die Puppe ein kleines Festgewand und wird gleichfalls eingeweiht. Wenn ein Kind gestorben ist, wird niemand von seinem Tod sprechen. Man würde sagen, dass sie im heiligen Hain verschwunden ist, um nach seinem Geschwisterteil zu suchen.

61
DIE GROSSE FEIER Mahounon bei den dreitägigen Feierlichkeiten anlässlich der Bekanntgabe von Gounon als Nachfolger im Amt des Oberpriesters. Voodoo-Geistliche aus ganz Benin sind angereist, um ihre Glückwünsche zu überbringen.

DIE DUNKELHEIT
BESUCH IN DER VORHÖLLE

62
Ein Patient in einer Nervenklinik in Cotonou (Benin) gräbt ein Loch, in dem er sich zu verstecken wünscht. Er verfiel in Trance und kehrte seither nicht mehr zurück. Die Klinik hat kleine Häuser für 150 Patienten. Sie schauen in eine Welt, zu der uns der Zugang verwehrt ist.

71
¬LEGBA DER TRICKSTER Eines Tages vernahm die höchste Göttin Mahoulissa im Himmel das laute Schluchzen eines Menschenkindes. Berührt von seinem Schmerz, sandte sie ihren Sohn Legba, um ihn zu trösten. Legba folgte dem Schluchzen bis zu einem Palast. Dort, im Dunklen, stieß er auf einen jungen Prinzen, der bitterlich weinte. »Warum weinst du?«, fragte Legba. »Mein Vater ist tot, ich bin allein und weiß nicht, was aus mir werden soll«, schluchzte der Junge. »Was würdest du mir geben, wenn ich jemanden für dich finde, der dir von nun an und für alle Ewigkeit den Weg zeigt und dich beschützt?«, fragte Legba. »All meine Schätze«, antwortete der Prinz. Legba nahm den Jungen bei der Hand und führte ihn hinaus in die Sonne. Er zeigte zu Boden: »Da. Das ist dein Führer. Und jetzt gib mir deinen Schmuck.« Der Prinz protestierte: »Aber, das ist mein Schatten! Er war immer da! Er gehört mir! Das bin doch ich!« »Genau«, sagte Legba, packte des Prinzen Krone und Zepter und machte sich feixend davon.

DIE DUNKELHEIT
MAGIER & ZAUBERER

72
¬CHAKATOU Die Chakatou sind Zauberer, denen ihre Bestimmung durch ein außergewöhnliches Ereignis kundgetan wurde. So arbeitete Cosmé ursprünglich als Lokführer. Eines Tages passierte ein furchtbares Unglück: Er überlebte als einziger und... verstand sofort, dass er auserwählt war, den Willen der Götter zu befolgen. Zeremonien unter dem

Vorsitz der Chakatou erfordern wochenlange Vorbereitungen. Die nötigen Zutaten kauft man auf dem Fetischmarkt.

79

RAUCH Für die Chakatou ist Rauch eine Quelle von Kraft und Macht.

80

¬MAWUS WEGE SIND GERECHT Als Legba einmal durch die Welt reiste, traf er auf einen Mann, der sein Begleiter wurde. Er wusste nicht, dass Legba ein Gott war. Die Nacht verbrachten beide im Haus einer Familie. Eines der Kinder war sehr krank. Legba gab dem Vater etwas Pulver, das dieser dem Kranken verabreichte. Währenddessen eilte Legba zu seinem Gefährten: »Mach schnell! Wir müssen weg!« Als sie das Haus fluchtartig verließen, hörten sie die Familie rufen: »Wo ist der Fremde?« – Das Kind war tot.

In der darauf folgenden Nacht bezogen sie in einem anderen Haus Quartier. Als der Tag dämmerte, nahm Legba einen Feuerstein und machte Feuer und ... entzündete damit das Stroh. Sogleich riss er seinen Gefährten aus dem Schlaf: »Wach auf! Wir müssen los! Mach schnell!« Als sie flüchteten, stand das Haus lichterloh in Flammen. Die Menschen schrien: »Wo sind die Fremden, die das angerichtet haben?«

Der Gefährte war von Legbas Taten tief beschämt und wollte sich davon machen. Legba aber holte ihn ein. »Du bist verwundert darüber, was ich getan habe. Ich bin kein menschliches Wesen, ich bin Gott Legba, der Sohn von Mahoulissa. Sie hieß mich tun, was ich getan habe. Hätte ich das Kind nicht getötet, wäre es noch als Jugendlicher zum Mörder seiner Eltern geworden. Die Familie, der ich das Haus anzündete, hat viele reiche Mitglieder, die aber zu geizig sind, ihr Vermögen mit den Kindern zu teilen. Wenn man das Haus wieder aufbaut, werden die Kinder das versteckte Geld entdecken.«

»Wenn du im Laufe deines Lebens solche Dinge erlebst, dann weißt du, dass Mahoulissas göttlicher Wille am Werk ist.« ⚑

81

LEGBA Ein dem Gott Legba geweihter Schrein vor dem Eingang eines Hauses, um dieses vor Krankheiten, unreinen Geistern und dem Tod zu beschützen. Legba ist das Bindeglied zwischen Voodoo-Göttern und Menschen. Nichts geschieht ohne seine Einwilligung, und oft ist er launisch und grausam.

✳DIE DUNKELHEIT✳
GRIS-GRIS & ASSINS

84

FETISCHE sind heilige Objekte im Besitz von Heilern und Zauberern, die mit ihrer Hilfe mit den Göttern in Kontakt treten. Im Haus eines Gläubigen ist stets ein Zimmer, das den Toten gewidmet ist. Altäre stehen darin und Metallstäbe (Assin) mit Figuren, die den Ahnen geweiht sind. Die Toten werden in Ehren gehalten, sollen aber nicht in Angst und Schrecken versetzen. Sie führen und beschützen uns. Ein Kreuz als Krönung eines Assin verrät, dass ein Ahne zum Christentum übertrat.

92

Daniel Avoudjeman von Agonssa (Ouida) spricht unter Verwendung eines Fetischs einen Fluch aus. Gott Legba muss zu jedem Handel zwischen Sterblichen und Göttern seine Einwilligung geben.

93

¬LEGBA NARRT MAHOULISSA Es gab eine Zeit, da lebte die höchste Göttin Mahoulissa mit ihrem Sohn Legba auf der Erde. Wann immer etwas Gutes geschah, dankten die Menschen Mahoulissa, auch wenn es Legba zu

verdanken war. Wann immer etwas schief ging, machte sie ihren Sohn dafür verantwortlich. Langsam fingen die Menschen an, Legba zu hassen.

Mahoulissas ganzer Stolz war ein Garten, in dem sie Yams gepflanzt hatte. Legba erzählte ihr, dass Diebe alle Wurzeln zu stehlen beabsichtigten. Mahou rief die Menschen der Erde zusammen, um ihnen kundzutun, dass der erste, der in ihrem Garten etwas stehle, getötet werde. In jener Nacht regnete es. Legba ging zu Mahous Haus und stahl ihre Sandalen. Er zog sie an, ging in den Garten und klaute den Yams. Am nächsten Morgen wurde der Diebstahl entdeckt. Sofort ließ Mahou alle Leute in einer Reihe aufstellen, um zu sehen, zu wessen Füßen die Abdrücke im Schlamm passten. Aber es passte keiner.

Da sprach Legba: »Könnte es sein, dass Mahou in der Nacht selbst im Garten war und es vergessen hat?« Mahou schimpfte wutentbrannt, willigte aber ein, ihre Füße in die Abdrücke zu stellen. Sie passten genau. Wütend rief die Menge: »Hier ist eine Eigentümerin, die sich selbst bestiehlt!« Mahou ward gedemütigt vor ihrem Volk, und so zog sie sich in den Himmel zurück, fern der Mühsal der Erde, und überließ Legba seinem eigenen Tun. ⚑

✳DIE FETISCHE✳
TELEFON/FRUCHTBARKEIT/HOHO/SCHUTZ/WAHRSAGUNG

96

¬DAS TELEFON Um mit den Göttern zu kommunizieren, werden speziell gefertigte Telefone verwendet. Sie bestehen aus einer Flasche, worin sich eine Figur befindet, die den Besitzer des Telefons darstellt. Niemand stellt die Frage, wie die Figur in die Flasche hineinkam.

¬DER ANRUF Eine große Kaurischnecke wird am Flaschenhals angeklebt. Der Fuß der Flasche wird mit roten Stofffetzen (meistens von einem Kleidungsstück des Besitzers) umwickelt und mit zwei kleineren Kauris versehen, einer auf der linken und einer auf der rechten Seite.

Um ein Gebet an die Gottheit zu richten, müssen einige Tropfen des Parfüms, das man benutzt, in die Flasche gegeben werden. Dann wird diese mit beiden Händen gehalten, wobei die Daumen gegen die beiden Kauris am Flaschenfuß gedrückt werden. Dann setzt man die Lippen an die große Kauri am Flaschenhals und flüstert seinen Wunsch.

98

¬DER TRÄGER DER BOTSCHAFT Der bochio hat ein Loch im Bauch, in das der Bokounon das Gebet des Bittstellers hineinflüstert. Es kann ein gutes oder ein böses Gebet sein: ein Rachefluch, aber auch eine Bitte um Fruchtbarkeit. Nachdem er die Botschaft in das Loch geflüstert hat, setzt der Bokounon den Stift wieder ein. Genau jetzt setzt die Wirkung des Zaubers ein. An der Unterseite des bochio befindet sich ein Metalldorn, mit dem er in den Boden hineingesteckt werden kann. Der Ort, an dem der bochio aufgestellt wird, HÄNGT VON DER ART DER BOTSCHAFT AB. Es kann zum Beispiel ein abgelegener Pfad sein, der zum Markt führt, ein Feld oder ein Beratungszimmer des Fa-Orakels. Manchmal wird er auch heimlich unter ein Bett oder in eine besondere Kiste oder Truhe gestellt.

100

DER ›MIT MACHT AUFGELADENE LEICHNAM‹ ist schwer beladen mit kleinen Päckchen, die Substanzen mit magischen Kräften enthalten. Diese Päckchen werden mit Perlenschnüren, Lederriemen oder Fäden an der Figur befestigt. Obwohl unter ihrer Last fast verborgen, strahlt die reglose Figur große Ruhe aus. Sie gehört zu den kleineren Fetischen, gewiss aber auch zu den machtvollsten. Ein Blick unter ihren Rock zeigt, wie reich sie ausgestattet ist.

102

¬GLÜCKSGABEN Diese Hoho stellen keine Kinder, sondern Gottheiten dar. Wenn Zwillinge auf die Welt kommen, werden sie von den Eltern als Glücksboten betrachtet. Weil sie so selten sind, erhalten Zwillinge eine besondere Behandlung und werden nach strengen Regeln aufgezogen. Sie müssen alles gerecht untereinander teilen.

WENN EIN GESCHWISTERTEIL STIRBT, wird eine kleine Statue geschnitzt, die künftig an seine Stelle tritt. Die Mutter trägt sie immer mit sich umher. Nach einiger Zeit übernimmt das überlebende Geschwisterteil die Sorge für die Statue. Es teilt sein Essen mit ihr und kleidet sie wie sich selbst.

Zwillinge werden nicht unbedingt identisch dargestellt. Manchmal ist die eine Figur glatt und poliert, die andere rau und grob. AUCH WENN NUR EINES DER GESCHWISTER ÜBER MAGISCHE KRÄFTE VERFÜGT, weitet sich sein übernatürliches Wesen auch auf sein anderes Geschwisterteil aus.

104

Der Fetisch als Heilquelle.

105

Nägel als Schmerzmittel.

106

¬DAS HERZSTÜCK DES GANZEN Unter den grisgris, den Fetischen, kommt der Brust eine besondere Aufmerksamkeit zu. Weil mit dem Herzen verbunden, gilt die Brust oft als eine Quelle des Lebens. Die Fon kennen den Ausdruck ku hun, was »totes Herz« bedeutet. Er hat eine positive Bedeutung und besagt soviel wie Geduld, Gelassenheit und Ruhe.

Oft werden diese Fetische in großen Gruppierungen präsentiert, wobei der Brustbereich der einzelnen Figuren mit Nägeln durchstoßen oder mit Schnur oder anderem Material eng eingeschnürt ist. Obwohl von aggressivem Äußeren, werden diese Fetische für Heilzwecke verwendet. Ein erkrankter Ratsuchender schlägt einen Nagel in das Holz, und er wird geheilt.

109

¬DAS GESPIEGELTE BÖSE Dieser gris-gris schützt seinen Besitzer und fügt anderen, die ihm Böses wollen, Schaden zu. Im Fetisch befinden sich Haare und Nägel des Besitzers. Der Körper ist mit Metallstücken und Spiegelglas bedeckt. Diese beiden Materialien spüren Gefahr auf und wehren sie ab. Wird der Besitzer verflucht, werden die bösen Gedanken zum Absender zurückgespiegelt: Er wird von ihnen zerstört.

110

¬DIE HEILENDE FLASCHE Wie das Telefon bedarf auch die heilende Flasche eines reichlich bemessenen Spritzers des Parfüms des Besitzers, um aktiviert zu werden. Die Flasche enthält von ihm HAARE UND NÄGEL. Der weitere Inhalt bleibt ein Geheimnis. Dieses Exemplar zeigt das ROTE KREUZ-Symbol, weil alle Welt in ihm ein Zeichen für positive Kraft erkennt. Die Flasche gilt als Talisman, der den Reisenden schützt und ihm Glück bringt. Sie ist klein und bequem transportierbar.

113

¬FLASCHENPOST Diese assins stellen die Ahnen des Besitzers dar und schützen ihn vor seinen Feinden. Jeder, der versucht, dem Besitzer der Flasche einen Fluch zu schicken, riskiert selbst sein Leben.

114

¬DAS FA-ORAKELBRETT Der Bokounon hat Zugang zum Wissen über das Schicksal eines jeden Menschen, weil er das Fa lesen kann. Im System des Fa gibt es 256 (16 x 16) Zeichen. Das Schicksal, das jedem Kind in die Wiege gelegt wird, findet seine Entsprechung in einem dieser Zeichen. Dieses bleibt einem Menschen bis zu seinem Tod.

Der Bokounon kann das Fa auf zweierlei Weise lesen. Entweder wirft er sechzehn Kolanüsse auf eine Fläche und deutet das Schicksal eines Ratsuchenden nach der Anordnung der Nüsse, oder er benutzt dafür ein eigenes Brett. Die Hand der Ratsuchenden wird über eine Fläche, bedeckt mit weißem Pulver aus zermahlenen Knochen, geführt, auf der er Linien zieht. Meist debattiert eine Runde von Bokounons stundenlang über die Deutung der Linien, bevor sie dem Bittsteller einen Rat erteilen: eine recht aufwändige Prozedur.

✤DIE MACHT✤
PRIESTER/PRIESTERINNEN/NOVIZEN/INITIIERTE

118

Mahounon hatte eine Vorahnung, dass er vor der Zeit sterben würde, war doch sein Vater 116 Jahre alt geworden. Er befragte das Fa-Orakel, um seinen Nachfolger im Amt des Oberpriesters des Mawu-Lissa-Klosters zu finden. Schließlich erklärte das Fa, dass sein Nachfolger soeben das Alter von elf Jahren erreicht habe: Er besuche die Schule und lebe im Umkreis von fünfzig Kilometern. Man fand ein Kind, das zu Hoffnungen Anlass gab. Man wusste nun seinem Vater, dass es entsprechende Gaben hatte und berufen war. Dieser aber hielt sich für einen modernen Menschen und lehnte es ab, Priester des Voodoo zu werden. Nach drei Wochen war er gestorben.

Mit Unterstützung seines Großvaters wurde der Junge entführt. Die Behörden unternehmen in einem solchen Fall nichts. Er erhielt einen neuen Namen: Gounon (Gou ist der Gott des Eisens). Ab diesem Zeitpunkt war es nicht mehr statthaft, ihn bei seinem alten Namen zu nennen. Jetzt hatte er eine neue Familie. Mahounon wurde Gounons Vater, dessen Frau Gounons neue Mutter.

122

Die zehnjährige Na, Königin des Mahoulissa-Klosters.

125

Ein Achina-Hüter auf den Investitur-Feiern zu Ehren von Gounon.

127

Mahounon sinnt über einen Vorschlag des Klosterrates nach.

128

DAN, DIE REGENBOGENSCHLANGE Ein Voodoo-Anhänger vor dem Tempel von Dan, der heiligen Regenbogen-Schlange. Wie Mahoulissa ist auch Dan männlich und weiblich zugleich, Gott der Lüfte und des Firmaments. Ohne Anfang und ohne Ende, gebietet er/sie über Reichtum, Gelderwerb und Vergänglichkeit.

Beschließt er, einen Sterblichen mit Wohlstand zu segnen, nimmt er menschliche Gestalt an. Als Bettler verkleidet, belohnt er jene, die sich seiner voll Mitgefühl annehmen, mit Gold und Silber.

130

MAHINOU DÉHOUSSOU SANTOS aus dem Quartier Lébou in Ouidah hatte zwei Drillingsgeschwister, die bei der Geburt starben. Ihre Mutter befragte daraufhin das Fa-Orakel, welches verkündete, dass sich die Tochter in den Dienst an dem Voodoo-Gott Déhoussou stellen solle.

Den Déhoussou-Kult, der jeden Freitag an der Küste stattfindet, versehen ausschließlich Priesterinnen, die an ihren weißen Kopftüchern zu erkennen sind. Die Hingabe dieser Frau an Déhoussou ist so vollkommen, dass sie Haus und Hof verließ, ihre Kinder dem Ehemann übergab und sich ganz dem Gebet widmete.

136
¬OBERHAUPT DES VOODOO Daagbo Hounon ist Supreme Chief des Voodoo in Benin und offizieller Repräsentant des Kults. Er nimmt für sich in Anspruch, aus dem Meer zu kommen, wohin er bei seinem Ableben zurückkehrt. Sein Stab ruht in einem Kraftpunkt vor seinem Thron.

141
KPASSENON, KÖNIG VON OUIDAH UND HÜTER DES HEILIGEN HAINS, ist der eigentliche Hohepriester des Voodoo in Westafrika. Niemandem außer ihm ist der Zutritt zum heiligen Hain gestattet, den die Seelen der Toten bewohnen. Ein Kopfschmuck schützt sein Gegenüber vor der Kraft seines Blickes. Es heißt, dass man erblindet, wenn man Kpassenon direkt in die Augen schaut.

142
¬KPASSENON WIRD KÖNIG Kpassenon war ursprünglich Motorradmechaniker. Eines Nachts erschienen ihm zwei Leoparden im Traum und verkündeten ihm, er sei der neue König des heiligen Hains. Anderntags ging Kpassenon zum amtierenden König und erzählte seinen Traum. Der König verlangte einen Beweis, und also gingen beide in den Hain. Als sie vor einem gewaltigen Baum standen, kam mit einem Mal ein Sturm auf. Heftige Böen brachten den Baum zu Fall.
    Zwei Wochen später, am 14. Juli 1988, kehrten beide Männer an denselben Ort zurück. Wieder brach ein mächtiger Sturm aus. Sie warfen sich zu Boden, um nicht verletzt zu werden. Als sich der Sturm legte, stand der Baum wieder aufrecht. Dem König genügte dieses Zeichen als Beweis, und er erklärte Kpassenon zum neuen König und Hüter des heiligen Hains.

146
Kpassenon hat seine eigenen Adepten, die im Walde leben. Die Schmucknarben ihres Gesichts zeigen die Krallen des Leoparden. Aufgabe der Eingeweihten ist es, den Verstorbenen im heiligen Hain Gesellschaft zu leisten.

149
Kpassenon mit seiner weltlichen Kopfbedeckung.

151
Kpassenon sollte später in eines der höchsten Ämter des Voodoo in Benin gewählt werden.

152
DER KÖNIG DER YORUBA auf seinem Thron in Ouidah. Wie bei Kpassenon verhindert seine Kopfbedeckung, dass andere an seinem Blick erblinden. Der zweite Thron ist Gästen vorbehalten, die dadurch die gegenüberliegende Wand anschauen statt den König.

154
Dako Wêgbé Nestor von Bohicon ist ein traditioneller Heiler, Premier und Justizminister des Königs Dako. In seinem Wohnzimmer empfängt er Gäste.

156
KAHOULA Alpha Ousseni ist traditioneller Heiler in der Stadt Parakou. Mit seinem Fetisch (kahoula) gewährt er Reisenden eine sichere Heimkehr. Eine weitere seiner Spezialitäten ist die Heilung der Zuckerkrankheit.

157
Legbanon Gandoto Fandi ist der Hüter des Agadje-Legba-Schreins im Quartier Fonssalamé von Ouidah, in dem sich der mächtigste Legba-Altar von Benin befindet. In früheren Zeiten sollen hier – Quelle seiner Macht – Kindersklaven lebendig begraben worden sein.

159
DIE ZAUBERIN ZANGBAN ist 85 Jahre alt und nahezu blind. Von der Gemeinschaft gefürchtet, lebt sie allein. Vor ihrem Tod wird sie ihre Kräfte auf eine andere Frau übertragen: Hierbei wird die Jüngere keine Wahl haben. Auch ihr wird diese Kraft bis an ihr Lebensende zur Verfügung stehen.

✳ DIE MACHT✳
AMAZONEN

161
Eine Linsouhoulé ist die Wiedergeburt einer Amazone der Vergangenheit, Mitglied jenes weiblichen Reiterheeres, das aus den mutigsten Kämpferinnen der königlichen Armee bestand. Die Gefangenen, die diese Amazonen machten, wurden als Sklaven an europäische Händler verkauft (die schönsten behielten sie). Die Uniform der Amazonen zeigt königliche Embleme, u.a. Dolch und Säbel. In offizieller Tracht ist es ihnen nicht gestattet, das Kloster zu verlassen und berührt zu werden. Sie tragen keinen Narbenschmuck, leben nur zeitweise im Kloster und haben die Erlaubnis zu heiraten. Kontakte zwischen Männern und Frauen sind im Kloster allerdings ausgeschlossen.

164
Der Ehemann einer Amazone (Linsouhoulé)

166
DIE VERSÖHNUNG Begleitet von zwei Leoparden, stieg der Herrscher des Himmels Mahoulissa eines Tages in Gestalt einer Frau hinab zur Erde. Dort traf sie auf einen König ohne Krone, der mit seinem Volk durch die Ödnis zog. Sie fragte ihn, warum sie nicht in ihrer Heimat seien, in seinem Königreich. Der König antwortete, dass eine große Hungersnot über sie gekommen sei und sie ihre Heimat auf der Suche nach Nahrung verlassen hätten. Was auch immer sie täten, um die Götter des Voodoo zu besänftigen, es sei nie das Richtige. Legba nehme zwar ihre Opfergaben, bestrafe sie aber dennoch mit Dürre, Pest und Schlimmerem. Er nahm ihre Frauen und stahl ihr Geld. Mahoulissa fragte: »Und dennoch ehrt ihr die Götter des Voodoo?« Der König nickte. Angesichts des Leids, das ihr böswilliger Sohn angerichtet hatte, begann Mahoulissa zu weinen. Und als ihre Tränen Staub und Steine in fruchtbare Felder und prächtige Bäume verwandelten, verstanden der König und sein Volk, wer die Frau wirklich war. »Ich werde euch drei Propheten senden«, sagte Mahoulissa. »Sie werden euch lehren, das Fa zu lesen, das Orakel, das euer Schicksal bestimmt. Dann werdet ihr selbst wissen, was ihr tun müsst, um die Götter zu besänftigen, und mein Sohn wird euch nichts mehr antun können. – Das Wissen um das Fa ist der Schlüssel zu eurer Freiheit. Ihr müsst es von Generation zu Generation weitergeben. Bis zum Ende der Welt.«▪

167
Agoli Agbo, der König von Abomey.

169
Der König mit einigen seiner 42 Frauen. Er trägt ein silbernes Sieb vor der Nase, um nicht dieselbe Luft wie seine Untertanen einzuatmen. Es ist ihm untersagt, den königlichen Bezirk zu verlassen. Besucher bedienen sich der Vermittlung seines Außenministers, um mit dem König zu sprechen. Stets tafelt er allein; auch darf er nie das Meer sehen. Vor seiner Thronbesteigung war er Polizist in Porto Novo.

«DEUX VOIX»

27

AVANT-PROPOS DE WIM WENDERS

¬DE LA MAGIE, EN NOIR ET BLANC Lorsque Alberto Venzago m'a montré son film Mounted by the Gods (alors inachevé) pour la première fois, j'y ai vu spontanément le « film d'un photographe », sans être sûr d'ailleurs que mes propos soient perçus comme élogieux — ce qu'ils étaient sans aucun doute, car le film photographiquement parlant est une pure merveille. Inversement, quand j'ai qualifié le présent recueil de « livre d'un cinéaste », Alberto manifestement m'en a tenu rigueur. J'espère pouvoir faire valoir ici qu'il s'agit dans les deux cas non pas d'un paradoxe, mais d'un compliment...

La photographie, qu'on le veuille ou non, a toujours quelque chose de « ponctuel », elle éclaire l'instant, fixe le coup d'œil. On peut dire que même les images de l'univers du vodou sont des instantanés de ce type. C'est d'ailleurs précisément ce qu'on attend d'un photographe de Magnum. Or quand on feuillette ce livre, qu'on pénètre dans ce monde hors du commun, tel qu'il émerge ici du noir, quelque chose de tout différent se produit : un net sentiment de durée. Dans leur enchaînement, ces images instaurent une notion autre que celle habituellement proposée par la photographie — la notion de temps.

C'est la narration, la mise en abyme d'une fiction, qui crée cette dimension. Mais par les images de ce livre, Venzago nous raconte-t-il une histoire ? Le livre et le film ne sont-ils pas des « documents » ? Ou alors des inventions ? Peut-on regarder le film ou le livre et « en croire ses yeux » ? Connaître un peu les origines du film et de ces photos peut réellement nous éclairer.

Il y a quinze ans, en avril 1988 exactement, Venzago décide de traverser le continent africain en Vespa. Il travaille pour le compte de GEO. Les pistes, couvertes de nids-de-poule, disparaissent sous les pluies torrentielles. Les pannes se multiplient. Pour finir, la Vespa rend l'âme à Ouidah, au Bénin. Alberto prend en photo le mur plein de graffiti devant lequel il est contraint de faire halte. Il ne sait pas encore que ce mur abrite un célèbre monastère vodou et que l'homme en boubou, gentil et bedonnant, qui propose au photographe égaré de l'aider, est Mahounon en personne, l'un des prêtres vodou les plus influents d'Afrique occidentale et lui-même à la tête du monastère. Un peu plus tard, Mahounon lit un oracle au photographe suisse — c'est le début de sa fascination pour le vodou : ce qu'il vient d'entendre, sur son passé, sur sa propre vie, pour l'entendement humain, le prêtre ne peut d'aucune manière en avoir eu connaissance.

Ces deux hommes très différents se lient d'amitié ; une relation de confiance s'établit. Venzago pourra commencer le tournage deux ans plus tard et poursuivra ce travail pendant plus de douze ans. Tout au long de cette période, il se rend au Bénin, où il est autorisé à assister à des cérémonies et rituels que personne avant lui n'avait eu le droit de filmer, et que personne sans doute ne reverra avec tant d'authenticité. Ce film, Alberto l'a réussi pour ainsi dire « à la dernière seconde », dans un ultime moment d'innocence de cette partie du monde.

Il vivra ainsi une histoire étonnante : Mahounon pressent sa mort, bien avant l'heure, puisqu'il est encore dans ses meilleures années. Il a hâte de trouver à temps un successeur qu'il initiera aux secrets de ses fonctions. De tout le pays, des enfants sont amenés au monastère, mais après une année harassante de noviciat, aucun n'est retenu par Fâ, l'oracle du vodou. En revanche, tous les signes indiquent un garçon de 12 ans du village voisin : Gounon.

La mère refusant d'envoyer son fils au monastère, il lui est retiré d'office. Venzago a filmé les quatre années de formation de Gounon, son initiation aux secrets de la religion. Le professeur transmet au jeune garçon tout ce qu'un grand prêtre doit savoir : magie noire, magie blanche, danses extatiques, action mystérieuse de l'oracle.

Mahounon meurt, de fait, soudainement et prématurément. Alberto est là, avec sa caméra, lorsque Gounon est sur le point d'être désigné, trop jeune au fond, trop peu préparé pour suivre les traces de son maître. À l'issue d'épreuves difficiles, le jeune de 17 ans est cependant reconnu par toutes les sommités locales du vodou. Dans une cérémonie solennelle, le roi du pays l'introduit dans le cercle des grands prêtres.

Plus on est saisi par l'attrait de cette histoire, plus on la saisit comme une fiction. D'aucuns trouveront ce monde trop féerique, trop invraisemblable à nos yeux et pour notre époque. Dans le film, comme dans le livre, Venzago s'interdit toute interprétation. Il ne livre aucune explication ethnologique, il montre seulement ce qu'il voit, de façon phénoménologique. Pourtant, il n'abandonne pas les images à elles-mêmes : il y juxtapose des fables et mythes de l'univers vodou, récités par un imposant conteur qui envoûte le spectateur de sa voix.

C'est ainsi qu'on apprend, en passant, tout ce qui est nécessaire pour suivre l'histoire de Mahounon et Gounon ; ces êtres, issus d'une étrange cosmogonie, nous permettent de soulever un coin de voile sur cette religion.

Le livre renferme lui aussi la narration, dont l'impact est tout autre que dans le film. Car Venzago a réussi à transformer la contemplation des images et la lecture des textes en une aventure filmique. Un rythme se crée qui met le papier en mouvement, qui donne l'impression que ces photos en noir et blanc tournoient : les états de transe, immortalisés en lui, sont autrement plus vivants et plus réels qu'ailleurs, dans d'autres livres de photos. (Le film réussit lui aussi quelque chose de magique : la couleur émerge de ce monde en noir et blanc et disparaît de nouveau sans que les transitions se remarquent.)

Pour s'abandonner à ce livre, pour se laisser porter par lui comme au cinéma, je conseille de mettre la bande son le plus fort possible. Venzago et ses musiciens, Boris Blank, Peter Scherer et Jochen Schmidt-Hambrock, ont osé en effet quelque chose d'audacieux : à partir de prises de son réelles des danses et des cérémonies, ils créent une musique contemporaine d'un genre nouveau, faite d'échantillons et de boucles qui contiennent toute l'ambiance et le tourbillon de la musique originale. Mais celle-ci est simultanément « traduite », pour qu'elle nous soit plus proche, qu'elle nous rentre davantage dans la peau que le son ethnologiquement correct.

C'est précisément la force de ce travail, véritable œuvre globale d'images et de sons : il nous rentre dans la peau. Ce qu'on a vu, ce qu'on a entendu, il est difficile de s'en débarrasser. Trop de choses sont inexplicables, et pas seulement le mélange de fiction et de réalité, de simulé et d'authentique, de jumbo gonflable et de regards d'enfants épuisés de fatigue.

Plus je connais le livre et le film, moins j'arrive à dire de quoi ils relèvent. En ce sens, je retire mes définitions initiales — sans doute à ton grand soulagement, Alberto. Mais je sais une chose avec certitude : ce que tu as distillé à partir de ces douze années insolites, de ces plus de cent heures de matériel vidéo et de ces milliers de négatifs, n'a jamais existé auparavant, ni au cinéma, ni dans la photographie — c'est tout simplement unique.

35

ALBERTO VENZAGO

PRIVATE OBSESSION, PUBLIC AFFAIR Allada, Abéokouta, Afagnagan : joyau de noms qui s'égrènent. Collier de perles fait de noms de ville où chaque pierre est un village. Dassa, Savinou, Kilkibo, Parakou, Ouidah : noms de petits États et de petits royaumes qui font rêver les humains, à commencer par moi-même !

Nous sommes au printemps 1988. Cette fois, mon voyage ne devait pas avoir d'objectif. Je voulais apprendre l'autre Afrique, celle de ma jeunesse. Je sens encore l'odeur des pages jaunies de vieux livres d'images parlant d'explorateurs, de zones en pointillé noir et blanc délimitant d'immenses étendues de forêts vierges, d'animaux encore jamais vus, de puissants rapides et de chutes d'eau de la hauteur d'un clocher. Je voulais retrouver ce sentiment d'aventure. Je voulais vivre l'inimaginable.

Après des années de reportages sur les opprimés et les puissants, je ne connaissais l'Afrique jusque-là qu'en tant que spécialiste de l'horreur. Mes photographies de cette époque montrent des corps bannis crevant de faim, des despotes à la mine sombre suite au dernier coup d'État ou des scènes d'un romantisme exacerbé conforme au cliché de « l'homme sauvage ». J'enfourche donc ma Vespa et pars. Sans but. Sans contrainte de temps. Tout simplement pour traverser l'Afrique. À la recherche de quelque chose d'inconnu.

J'ai trouvé ce que je cherchais lorsque je fus contraint de m'arrêter. Un ennui de moteur me tint cloué à Ouidah, une petite ville du Bénin, en Afrique de l'Ouest. C'est ainsi que je fis la connaissance de Mahounon, l'un des grands prêtres vodoun d'Afrique. Commençait alors pour moi un long voyage spirituel.

Naturellement, à ce moment-là, tout cela me parut fortuit. En fin de compte, il aurait tout aussi bien pu m'arriver quelque chose d'extraordinaire au Togo ou au Ghana ou n'importe où ailleurs, pensais-je à l'époque.

Le Bénin, autrefois royaume du Dahomey, était une Sparte noire coincée entre les peuples des Yorubas, dans le Nigéria actuel, et d'Ife, implantés au Ghana occidental et au Togo. D'après la légende, la lignée royale du Dahomey descend d'une princesse originaire d'Adja et d'un léopard qui la séduisit sur les bords du fleuve Mono. Dès lors, les rois de ce pays se firent des scarifications sur les tempes pour rappeler les griffes de l'animal.

Les guerriers farouches du Dahomey étaient des femmes, leur principale source de revenus était l'asservissement et le commerce des peuples voisins vaincus, réduits en esclavage. Traditionnellement, à la mort du roi, son successeur devait faire la guerre pour assujettir de nouvelles tribus, car il était de son devoir d'augmenter la richesse de son pays.

Le culte vodoun est né dans ces contrées, frappées par les guerres et les razzias, qui devaient ultérieurement devenir tristement célèbres sous l'appellation de côte des Esclaves. Il fut ensuite exporté dans le monde entier par les esclaves. Avec la fin de l'esclavage, le Bénin tomba dans l'oubli. Quasiment dépourvu de richesses naturelles, comme le pétrole ou les diamants, et sans importance géopolitique par rapport à ses voisins bien plus imposants, le pays tomba dans l'oubli, et pendant longtemps le progrès ne s'y fit guère sentir. C'est pourquoi la vie s'y écoulait encore de façon très primitive.

Bien qu'il ait été combattu par des missionnaires de toutes religions et des hommes politiques de toutes couleurs, le vodou est resté fortement ancré dans la culture béninoise. 35 % des Béninois sont chrétiens, 25 % musulmans, tandis que les adeptes du vodou représentent 80 %. Ces statistiques sont moins le résultat d'un recensement contestable qu'une preuve de la merveilleuse tolérance des Africains envers la religion.

Avec l'aide de Mahounon, je plongeais dans un autre monde : Il me parla de la vie au couvent et m'autorisa à participer à des cérémonies tenues secrètes. J'étais avant tout fasciné par l'innocence des hommes. Depuis, je passe chaque année quelques mois là-bas.

Sans aucun bagage anthropologique, je m'étais lancé dans un voyage vers l'inconnu. Je voulais plutôt abandonner cette tendance à vouloir trouver des réponses toutes faites. « Une quantité de paroles ne remplit pas un panier », dit un proverbe du Ghana.

Je me sens bien chez ces gens. Chaque visite m'ouvre de nouvelles portes. L'inconnu me devient plus familier et pourtant plus je suis là et plus je pense connaître les rites, plus les adeptes du vodou me font sentir que je ne sais encore rien. La confiance n'est pas accordée d'emblée, elle se gagne.

Presque imperceptiblement, je sentis au fil des ans que s'installait une passerelle entre mes deux grandes passions : la photographie et mon intérêt pour les rites. Dans ces domaines, je voulais essayer de ne pas simplifier, et de ne pas tomber dans les lieux communs, les clichés et les semi-vérités.

Un jour, Mahounon m'expliqua que je n'étais pas venu en Afrique pour vivre une aventure, mais que c'était lui qui était venu me chercher pour que son histoire soit connue. Comme toujours, le résultat prit douze années de travail, qui déboucha sur un film, un CD et ce livre.

L'été bat son plein lorsque j'assiste aux cérémonies de funérailles de Mahounon. Dans la chambre funéraire, il fait complètement noir. Pendant que j'évalue la faible lumière, les grands prêtres commencent la cérémonie. À reculons, penchés en avant, ils se déplacent lentement, avec une chèvre et une poule, au son des tam-tams tandis que dehors, la communauté du couvent chante et danse dans une chaleur suffocante. J'aimerais commencer à filmer lorsque Kpassenon et les prêtres du nouveau culte Mahou Lissa me font passer un fétiche. Pendant ces neuf années, je suis toujours resté un journaliste. Je n'ai jamais réussi à franchir le cap qui m'aurait fait passer d'observateur à participant. Et, hormis Pierre Verger, aucun blanc n'est jamais devenu un Fatumbi, un prêtre vodou, un initié, celui qui sait. À ce moment-là, je suis partie prenante de la cérémonie. Filmer devient secondaire.

La prophétie de Mahounon s'est accomplie : Gounon a été intronisé comme son successeur. Les mouchoirs en papier et les télévisions couleur ont fait leur entrée dans ce monde préservé. Ouidah a complètement changé de visage. Ses habitants également. L'amitié cependant n'est pas brisée, même si le film et le livre sont terminés. Elle demeure.

Ce livre n'est pas un livre spécialisé. C'est une invitation au voyage. Un voyage aux sources du vodou, une invitation à faire connaissance avec Kpassenon, le gardien des forêts sacrées, et Aboli Ahgbo, le roi d'Abomey avec ses 42 femmes. Avec le mage Fofo, le rival détesté condamné, par télépathie, à une éternelle érection, avec Gounon qui, du haut de ses vingt et un ans, doit assumer la charge de tout un monastère. Avec des paysages encore préservés des hordes de touristes. Avec des hommes enracinés dans la foi.

Mes remerciements vont à tous mes amis de Ouidah, notamment à Lambert Abagadan, responsable des prises de vue, qui m'a montré une Afrique qui est bien davantage qu'une image dans un livre d'enfant, l'artiste Yves Pede, la traductrice Martine de Souza, mon ami vodou Gounon Tokpo, Kpassenon, le gardien des forêts sacrées qui m'appelle « mon prince », Fofo et toute la famille de Mahounon. Ils ont tous une place dans mon cœur.

Un merci tout particulier à Thilo Rösheisen qui non seulement m'a apporté pour ce projet un soutien précieux avec ses idées et ses textes, mais a surtout toujours été à mes côtés un ami de bon conseil. Je remercie Kit Hopkins pour son soutien indéfectible et son inspiration pendant toutes ces années, depuis le début de mon obsession. À partir des légendes et des récits que j'ai recueillis tel un chasseur et un collectionneur, elle a écrit le magnifique texte du film et du livre.

Je me suis également fait des amis en dehors de l'Afrique. Wim et Donata Wenders sont entrés dans ma vie. Je suis reconnaissant et heureux qu'ils soient là. Wim a soutenu ce projet en tant que producteur exécutif et m'a témoigné sa confiance dans la force des images. Le livre est prêt. 125 photographies, prises au 1/125 secondes. Cela fait au total une seconde. Une seconde à Ouidah : bien peu de temps. Mais qu'est ce que le temps en Afrique. « Il y a trois jours », me disait toujours Mahounon — même quand nous ne nous étions pas vus depuis un an.

PRIS PAR LES DIEUX
Kit Hopkins

∗L'OBSCURITÉ∗
PEOPLESCAPE

44

LES ABIKOUS DE DJOHITIN Si une femme fait une fausse couche, elle demande conseil aux Abikous. Elle leur offre un ballot d'étoffes. Si elle est de nouveau enceinte et qu'elle met au monde un enfant sain, elle doit présenter le bébé aux Abikous qui le marque d'un signe sur la joue. Ensuite, chaque année, la mère devra leur apporter de l'argent, de la nourriture, même une chèvre entière. Sinon, elle aura des problèmes.

Les Abikous passent pour très dangereux. Les villageois vivent dans la crainte qu'ils s'adressent à eux : « Aidez-moi ! Mes vêtements sont vieux et sales. Aidez-moi ! », implorent-ils. Les Abikous ont des voix très aiguës, ils parlent soit le fon soit le yorouba. Ils ne peuvent sortir que le jour. Ils n'ont pas le droit à l'obscurité.

46

LES GARDIENS ACHINA visitent le couvent Mahou-Lissa de Mahounon et attendent de faire leur visite de politesse à Gounon. (Achina, à gauche au fond, est le « Graal » du vodou.)

50

LA GENÈSE Un jour, notre Terre fut plongée dans les ténèbres et le chaos, le feu détruisit nos forêts. Les océans s'emportèrent et les cieux cessèrent de faire tomber la pluie. Les femmes enceintes donnèrent naissance à des cabris et non à des enfants. Les points d'eau s'asséchèrent, le sol devint aussi dur que la pierre. Il n'y eut plus de récoltes. Les mères, impuissantes devant la mort de leurs enfants, devinrent folles.

Partout, les hommes se battaient, car chacun accusait l'autre d'avoir causé ces calamités. Désespérés, les aînés se réunirent pour trouver une solution. Hélas ! la souffrance persista. ∎

Un jour, une femme apparut parmi nous. Elle venait du pays Adja. C'était une femme sage, guidée par deux léopards. Elle regarda notre Terre de chaos et de ténèbres et dit au Roi : « Vos souffrances ne cesseront que si vous adorez les dieux du vodou comme nous le faisons. »

MAHOU-LISSA L'homme-femme Mahou-Lissa, dieu suprême et gouverneur des Cieux, est une créature à deux visages : l'un est celui d'une femme, ses yeux sont la Lune. L'autre est celui d'un homme, ses yeux sont le Soleil. Mahou commande la nuit, et Lissa, le jour.

Comme Mahou-Lissa est pareillement homme et femme, elle enfanta. Elle répartit l'Univers parmi ses nombreux enfants : la Terre revint à l'aîné, les cieux aux jumeaux, les océans au cadet et ainsi de suite.

Mais rien ne resta pour le benjamin Legba, son enfant préféré. Elle en fit donc son messager. Lui seul peut communiquer avec tous les êtres, terrestres et célestes. Il peut être cruel et malfaisant. Les grâces de Legba s'obtiennent par le sacrifice — le sacrifice du sang.

57

LEGBASSI La tâche de cette jeune adepte du vodou consiste à distraire l'assistance pendant les trois jours des cérémonies Legbassi. Les noix de cola qu'elle a dans la bouche doivent être coupées en 16 morceaux. Elles sont utilisées pour l'oracle Fâ.

58/60

LES POUPÉES EN BOIS représentent des jumeaux ou le frère ou la sœur d'un jumeau d'une adepte du vodou morts généralement à la naissance. La mère garde la poupée (ou même plusieurs) jour et nuit avec elle : l'esprit de l'enfant mort continue de vivre en elle. Elle sait que si elle oublie ou perd la poupée, quelque chose de terrible se passera. La poupée fait tout comme elle. Quand le temps d'une cérémonie d'initiation est venu, la poupée porte un petit vêtement de cérémonie ; elle aussi est initiée. Quand un enfant est mort, personne ne parlera de sa mort. On dira qu'elle a disparu dans la forêt sacrée en cherchant son jumeau.

61

LA GRANDE CÉRÉMONIE Mahounon lors des trois jours de cérémonie annonçant que Gounon reprendra les fonctions de grand prêtre. Les dignitaires vodou viennent de tout le Bénin pour transmettre leurs félicitations.

∗L'OBSCURITÉ∗
VISITE À LIMBO

62

Un patient à l'asile d'aliénés de Cotonou (Bénin) creuse un trou dans lequel il veut se cacher. Il est rentré en transe et n'en est plus jamais ressorti. L'hôpital a des bungalows pour 150 patients. Ils sont tournés vers un monde auquel nous n'avons pas accès.

71

¬LEGBA L'ESPIÈGLE Un jour, dans les cieux, la déesse suprême Mahou-Lissa entendit un jeune homme pleurer. Touchée, elle envoya son fils Legba le consoler. Legba suivit les sanglots jusqu'à un palais. Il y trouva un jeune prince pleurant dans le noir.
« Pourquoi pleures-tu ? », demanda Legba.
« Mon père est mort, je n'ai plus personne. Je suis seul et ne sais ce qui adviendra de moi », se plaignit le garçon « Que me donnes-tu en échange de quelqu'un qui veillera sur toi pour toujours ? », s'enquit Legba.
« Tous mes joyaux », répondit le prince.
Legba prit le garçon par la main, le mena à la lumière du soleil et pointa le sol. « Là. Voilà ton guide. Maintenant, donne-moi tes bijoux ! »
Le prince objecta : « Mais c'est mon ombre ! C'est la mienne ! Elle a toujours été ici ! C'est moi-même ! »
« Exactement », dit Legba, qui s'empara de la couronne et du sceptre, et détala.

72

¬CHAKATOUS Les Chakatous sont des sorciers dont la vocation a été révélée par un événement extraordinaire. Cosmé était anciennement conducteur de train. À la suite d'un terrible accident, il fut le seul survivant. Il savait ce que cela signifiait : il avait été choisi pour exécuter la volonté des dieux. Les cérémonies des Chakatous requièrent des semaines de préparation. Tous les ingrédients s'achètent sur le marché aux fétiches.

79

FUMÉE Les Chakatous considèrent la fumée comme une source de force et de pouvoir.

80

¬LES VOIES DE MAHOU SONT JUSTES Un jour, en parcourant la Terre, Legba rencontra un homme qui devint son compagnon de voyage. Celui-ci ne savait pas que Legba était un dieu. Ils passèrent tous deux la nuit dans la maison d'une famille dont l'enfant était très malade. Legba donna au père une poudre pour l'enfant malade puis se tourna vers son compagnon : « Vite ! Allons-nous en ! » Ils partirent en courant et entendirent la famille crier : « Qui est cet étranger ? » L'enfant était mort.

La nuit suivante, ils firent halte dans une autre maison. À la tombée du jour, Legba prit un silex et fit du feu. Il incendia la maison de paille où il avait dormi, puis se précipita vers son compagnon : « Lève-toi ! Nous devons partir ! Vite ! » Une fois qu'ils furent partis, la maison disparut dans les flammes. Les gens hurlèrent : « Où sont les étrangers qui ont fait ça ? »

Le compagnon avait honte de ce que Legba avait fait et tenta de fuir. Legba le rattrapa. « Tu t'étonnes de ce que j'ai fait. Je ne suis pas un être humain, je suis le dieu Legba, fils de Mahou-Lissa. Elle m'a envoyé faire ce que j'ai fait. Si je n'avais pas entraîné cet enfant dans la mort, il aurait tué ses propres parents avant d'être adulte. La famille dont j'ai incendié la maison a beaucoup de parents riches. Mais ils sont trop avares pour partager leur fortune avec les enfants. Quand ils reconstruiront la maison, les enfants trouveront l'argent caché. »

« Quand dans ta vie tu verras de telles choses, tu sauras que c'est la volonté divine de Mahou-Lissa qui agit. » ▉

81

Une châsse dédiée au dieu Legba, à l'entrée d'une maison pour la protéger des maladies, des mauvais esprits et de la mort. Legba fait le lien entre les dieux et les hommes. Rien ne peut être fait sans son consentement et il est souvent lunatique et cruel.

84

LES FÉTICHES sont les objets sacrés utilisés par les guérisseurs et les sorciers pour communiquer avec les dieux. Dans chaque maison, une pièce est consacrée aux morts. Elle est remplie d'autels et de baguettes métalliques (assins) dédiés aux ancêtres. Les morts doivent être adulés et respectés sans crainte. Ils nous guident et nous protègent. La croix apposée sur un assin indique la conversion d'un ancêtre au christianisme.

92

Daniel Avoudjeman de Agonssa (Ouidah) utilise un fétiche pour énoncer une malédiction. Le dieu Legba doit approuver tout échange entre les mortels et les dieux.

93

¬LA RUSE DE LEGBA ENVERS MAHOU-LISSA Il fut un temps où la déesse suprême Mahou-Lissa et son fils Legba vécurent ensemble sur Terre.

Chaque fois que quelque chose de bien se passait, les gens remerciaient Mahou-Lissa, même si Legba en était à l'origine. Chaque fois que quelque chose de mal se passait, elle blâmait son fils. Les gens se mirent à détester Legba.

Mahou-Lissa avait un jardin planté d'ignames. Legba lui dit que des voleurs envisageaient de les prendre. Mahou rassembla alors tous les gens de la Terre pour leur dire que le premier qui viendrait voler dans son jardin serait tué.

Une nuit, il plut. Legba se rendit à la maison de Mahou et lui prit ses sandales. Il les chaussa, alla dans le jardin et vola toutes les ignames. Le lendemain matin, le vol fut constaté. Legba fit rassembler tous les gens pour voir quels pieds correspondaient aux empreintes. Mais on ne trouva personne dont les pieds allaient dans les empreintes.

Legba dit alors : « Il est possible que Mahou elle-même soit passée par là et l'ait oublié ? » Mahou protesta, disant que c'était absurde, mais accepta de mettre son pied dans l'empreinte. Cela correspondait parfaitement. La foule en colère hurla : « Voici une propriétaire elle-même voleuse ! »

Mahou était humiliée. Elle savait qu'elle avait été dupée par son propre fils. Elle monta très haut dans les cieux, laissant Legba à ses affaires. ▉

96

LE TÉLÉPHONE Pour communiquer avec les dieux, il faut des téléphones spécialement conçus à cet effet, c'est-à-dire une bouteille contenant une figurine qui représente le propriétaire du téléphone. Personne ne cherche à savoir comment la figurine est rentrée dans la bouteille.

¬L'APPEL Un gros cauri est accroché au goulot de la bouteille. Le bas de la bouteille est enveloppé de chiffons rouges (venant généralement d'un vêtement du propriétaire) et deux cauris plus petits sont placés de part et d'autre.

Pour adresser une prière à la divinité, quelques gouttes du parfum utilisé par le propriétaire doivent être versées dans la bouteille. Celle-ci est prise ensuite entre les deux mains, de manière à ce que les pouces soient posés sur les petits cauris. On applique ensuite les lèvres sur le gros cauri et murmure son vœu.

98

¬LE MESSAGER Le bochio a un trou dans le ventre dans lequel le Bokounon murmure la prière de celui qui en fait la demande. La prière peut être bonne ou mauvaise — appel à la vengeance ou désir de fertilité. Une fois le message murmuré dans le trou, le Bokounon remet la tige. À ce moment précis, la magie fait effet. En bas du bochio se trouve une pointe de métal qui peut être rentrée dans le sol. L'endroit où est le bochio dépend de la nature du message. Ça peut être un sentier détourné qui conduit au marché, un champ ou une pièce de consultation de l'oracle Fâ. Parfois il est posé en cachette sous un lit ou dans une caisse particulière.

100

LE « CADAVRE CHARGÉ DE POUVOIR » est bardé de petits paquets contenant des substances aux pouvoirs magiques. Ces petits paquets sont fixés au personnage au moyen de cordelettes avec des perles, de courroies en cuir ou de fils. Bien que presque complètement dissimulé sous ce qu'il porte, le personnage inerte dégage une grande tranquillité. Il fait partie des fétiches les plus petits, mais assurément aussi les plus puissants. Un regard sous le vêtement révèle la richesse des parures.

102

AMULETTES Ces Hoho ne représentent pas des enfants mais des divinités. Des jumeaux qui viennent au monde sont considérés comme messagers du bonheur par leurs parents. Les jumeaux sont tellement rares qu'ils bénéficient d'un traitement particulier et sont éduqués selon des règles strictes. Ils doivent tout partager de manière équitable.

Lorsqu'un des jumeaux meurt, une petite statue ciselée le remplace. La mère la porte toujours sur soi. Au bout d'un certain temps, c'est au jumeau vivant de veiller sur la statuette, qui partage alors les repas et porte les mêmes vêtements.

Les jumeaux ne sont pas forcément représentés de façon identique. Parfois une figurine est lisse et polie, l'autre rêche et grossière. Même si l'un des jumeaux seulement a des pouvoirs magiques, ses dispositions surnaturelles rejaillissent sur l'autre.

104

Le fétiche comme source de guérison.

105

Des clous contre la douleur.

106

¬AU CŒUR DE TOUT Parmi les gris-gris, ou fétiches, la poitrine bénéficie d'une attention toute particulière. Proche du cœur, elle est considérée comme source de vie. Les Fon ont une expression : ku hun, qui signifie « cœur mort ». Elle a une signification positive, un peu comme patience, calme et sérénité.

Souvent, ces fétiches sont regroupés pour être présentés ; la poitrine de chacune des figurines est percée de clous ou fortement serrée avec une corde ou autre. Bien que d'apparence agressive, ces fétiches servent à favoriser les guérisons. Un malade en quête de soutien rentre un clou dans le bois, il est guéri.

109

¬LE REFLET DU MAL Ce gris-gris protège son propriétaire et s'en prend à ceux qui lui veulent du mal. Dans le fétiche se trouvent des cheveux et des ongles du propriétaire. Le corps est couvert de morceaux de métal et de verre. Ces deux matériaux guettent le danger et le repoussent. Si le propriétaire est maudit, les mauvaises pensées sont renvoyées à l'expéditeur : il sera détruit par eux.

110

¬LA BOUTEILLE QUI GUÉRIT Tout comme le téléphone, la bouteille qui guérit ne peut servir que si elle contient une bonne dose du parfum du propriétaire, de même que des cheveux et ongles à lui. Le reste du contenu est secret. Cet exemplaire présente le symbole de la Croix-Rouge, car le monde entier voit en lui le signe d'une force positive. La bouteille passe pour un talisman qui protège le voyageur et lui porte bonheur. Elle est petite et facile à transporter.

113

UNE « BOUTEILLE À LA MER » Ces assins représentent les ancêtres du propriétaire et le protègent de l'ennemi. Celui qui voudrait envoyer une malédiction au propriétaire de la bouteille risque sa propre vie.

114

¬LA PLANCHE DE L'ORACLE FÂ Le Bokounon peut tout savoir sur le destin de chaque humain parce qu'il peut lire le Fâ. Le système du Fâ se compose de 256 (16 x 16) signes. Le destin qui accompagne chaque enfant dès le berceau trouve sa correspondance dans l'un de ces signes, que l'individu conserve ensuite jusqu'à sa mort.

Le Bokounon peut lire le Fâ de deux manières. Soit il jette 16 noix de kola sur une surface et lit le destin de celui qui le demande selon l'agencement des noix ; soit il utilise pour ce faire une planche spéciale. La main du demandeur est guidée sur une surface recouverte d'une poudre blanche d'os broyés sur laquelle il trace des lignes. Généralement, un groupe de Bokounon discute pendant des heures de l'interprétation des lignes avant de donner conseil à celui qui le demande – une procédure difficile.

117

GOUNON:
mon père avait un don, une vocation. Mais il se considérait comme un homme moderne et refusa d'adhérer au vodou. Trois semaines plus tard, il était mort.

LA FORCE
PRÊTRES/PRÊTRESSES/NOVICES/INITIÉS
118

Mahounon eut la prémonition qu'il mourrait avant son heure. Son père avait atteint l'âge de 116 ans. Il consulta Fâ, l'oracle, pour trouver quelqu'un qui lui succéderait comme grand prêtre du couvent Mahou-Lissa. Finalement, Fâ déclara que le successeur de Mahounon avait 11 ans, qu'il fréquentait l'école et vivait dans un rayon de 50 kilomètres. On trouva un enfant qui paraissait prometteur. Son père était connu pour avoir eu des dons et une vocation, mais il se considérait comme un homme moderne et avait donc refusé de devenir prêtre vodoun. Il mourut dans les trois semaines qui suivirent.

Avec le soutien du grand-père, l'enfant fut enlevé à sa mère. Les autorités n'engagent aucune action dans un cas comme celui-là. On lui donna un nouveau nom : Gounon (Gou est le dieu du fer). Dès lors, personne n'eut le droit de prononcer son ancien nom. Il avait désormais une nouvelle famille. Mahounon devint le père de Gounon et la femme de Mahounon, sa mère.

122

Na, dix ans, reine du couvent Mahou-Lissa.

125

Un gardien Achina lors de la cérémonie d'investiture en l'honneur de Gounon.

127

Mahounon réfléchit à une décision du conseil du couvent.

128

DAN, LE SERPENT ARC-EN-CIEL Un adepte vodou devant le Temple de Dan, le serpent Arc-en-ciel. Comme Mahou-Lissa, Dan est à la fois homme et femme, dieu de l'Air et du Firmament. Il contrôle la fortune, les gains et la fugacité. S'il veut bénir un mortel par la prospérité, il prend une forme humaine. Déguisé en mendiant, il récompense avec de l'or et de l'argent ceux qui ont pitié de lui.

130

MAHINOU DÉHOUSSOU SANTOS, du quartier Lébou Ouidah, est l'un de trois enfants triplets. Les deux autres n'ayant pas survécu à la naissance, la mère de Mahinou alla consulter Fâ qui décida que sa fille se vouerait elle-même à la puissance vodou de Déhoussou. Seules

les femmes, reconnaissables à leurs foulards blancs, participent au culte Déhoussou qui a lieu chaque vendredi sur la plage. Sa dévotion à Déhoussou est telle qu'elle quitta sa maison et laissa ses enfants à son mari pour se donner entièrement à la prière.

136
CHEF SUPRÊME DU VOUDOU Daagbo Hounon, chef suprême du vodou au Bénin et représentant officiel du culte. Il se réclame comme venant de l'océan, où il retournera à sa mort. Son bâton se trouve à un point de gravité devant son trône.

141
KPASSENON, ROI DE OUIDAH ET GARDIEN DE LA FORÊT SACRÉE, est en Afrique occidentale le grand prêtre vodou par excellence. Nul excepté lui n'a le droit de pénétrer dans la Forêt sacrée, qui est habitée par les âmes des morts, sans la permission de Kpassenon. Sa parure sur la tête protège les autres de son regard. On dit que celui qui regarde Kpassenon dans les yeux devient aveugle.

142
KPASSENON DEVIENT ROI Kpassenon était à l'origine mécanicien, réparateur de Vespa. Une nuit, deux léopards porteurs de message lui apparurent en rêve : il serait le nouveau roi de la Forêt sacrée. Le jour suivant, Kpassenon se rendit chez le roi et gardien et lui raconta son rêve. Le roi voulut des preuves, alors ils entrèrent tous les deux dans la forêt. Comme ils se tenaient devant un grand arbre, une violente tempête se leva. L'arbre en fut déraciné. Deux semaines plus tard, le 14 juillet 1988, les deux hommes retournèrent au même endroit dans la forêt. Un autre orage éclata. Ils durent se coucher par terre pour se protéger. Lorsque le vent se calma, l'arbre était à nouveau debout.
Pour le vieux roi, la preuve était suffisante. Il déclara Kpassenon nouveau roi et gardien de la Forêt sacrée.

146
Kpassenon a ses propres initiés qui vivent dans les forêts. Les scarifications sur le visage représentent les griffes d'un léopard. Les initiés sont chargés de garder la compagnie des morts.

149
Kpassenon avec son couvre-chef séculier.

151 Kpasssenon allait être nommé plus tard à l'une des fonctions les plus élevées de la hiérarchie vodou au Bénin.

152
LE ROI DES YOROUBA sur son trône à Ouidah. Comme chez Kpassenon, sa parure sur la tête évite que ceux qui le regardent dans les yeux deviennent aveugles. Le trône à côté de lui est réservé aux invités, dont le regard est dirigé sur le mur opposé et non vers le roi.

154
Dako Wêgbé Nestor de Bohicon est guérisseur traditionnel, chancelier et ministre de la Justice du roi Dako. Il reçoit des invités dans son salon.

156
KAHOULA Alpha Ousseni est guérisseur traditionnel à Parakou. Avec son fétiche (kahoula), il garantit sécurité et succès aux voyageurs. Son autre spécialité est le diabète.

157
Legbanon Gandoto Fandi est gardien de la châsse Agadje Legba, dans le quartier de Fonssalamé (Ouidah), où se trouve le plus important autel de Legba au Bénin. C'est

ici, source de son pouvoir, que les esclaves d'enfants auraient jadis été enterrés vivants.

159
LA SORCIÈRE ZANGBAN a 85 ans, elle est presque aveugle. Très redoutée par la communauté, elle vit seule. Avant sa mort, elle transmettra son pouvoir à une autre femme, plus jeune, qui n'aura pas le choix : elle aussi aura ce pouvoir jusqu'à sa mort.

✝ LA FORCE ✝
AMAZONES

161
Une Linsouhoulé est la réincarnation d'une amazone du passé, membre d'une cavalerie féminine constituée des combattants les plus courageux de l'armée royale. Les prisonniers capturés par ces amazones étaient ensuite vendus comme esclaves à des marchands européens (elles gardaient les plus beaux pour elles). L'uniforme des amazones porte les insignes royaux, comme le poignard et le sabre. Tant qu'elles sont en uniforme, elles n'ont pas le droit de quitter le couvent et d'être touchées. Elles n'ont pas de scarifications, vivent seulement à temps partiel au couvent et sont autorisées à se marier. Toutefois, les contacts entre hommes et femmes sont interdits dans l'enceinte du couvent.

164
Le mari d'une amazone (Linsouhoulé).

166
LA RÉCONCILIATION Un jour, Mahou-Lissa, Dieu suprême et gouverneur des cieux, descendit sur Terre déguisé en femme et guidé par deux léopards. Là, elle rencontra le roi, sans couronne, qui marchait dans le désert avec ses sujets. Elle demanda pourquoi ils n'étaient pas à la cour. Le roi répondit qu'ils avaient souffert de la famine et ne trouvaient rien à manger malgré les offrandes faites aux dieux du vodou. En fait, Legba avait accepté leurs offrandes, mais les avait punis avec la sécheresse et d'autres fléaux ; pire encore, il avait pris leurs femmes et volé leur argent.
« Et vous adorez toujours les dieux du vodou ? » demanda Mahou-Lissa.
« Oui », répondit le roi.
Mahou-Lissa se mit à pleurer à cause de la méchanceté de son mauvais garçon. Et comme ses pleurs transformèrent les pierres et la poussière en plantes et en terres fertiles, le roi et ses sujets comprirent qui était vraiment cette femme.
« Je vous enverrai trois prophètes, dit Mahou-Lissa, et ils vous enseigneront le Fâ, l'oracle qui dicte votre destin. Ainsi, vous saurez honorer les dieux, et mon fils ne pourra plus vous faire de tort. C'est la clé de votre liberté. Vous devez la transmettre de génération en génération, jusqu'à la fin du monde. »

167/169
Agoli Agbo, roi d'Abomey, avec quelques-unes de ses 42 femmes. Il porte un couvre-nez argenté pour ne pas respirer le même air que ses sujets. Il n'a pas le droit de quitter la cour royale. Les visiteurs doivent passer par l'intermédiaire de son ministre de l'Extérieur pour s'adresser à lui. Il mange toujours seul et n'a pas le droit non plus de voir la mer.

Avant de prendre le trône, il était policier à Porto Novo.

¬ACKNOWLEDGMENTS

WITH THANKS TO MY ASSISTANTS OVER THE YEARS:
SERGE HÖLTSCHI — 1992; BEAT LENHERR — 1996/1997;
ALEXANDER KÜHNE — 1999/2000; SANDRA BERNASCONI — 2002;
BEATRICE MÜLLER — 1999/2000; BARBARA LÜTHI 2003;
LAMBERT ABADAGAN, OUIDAH — 1988-2003;
YVES PEDE, ABOMEY — 1996-2003

THANKS ALSO TO THILO RÖSCHEISEN
FOR HIS GENEROUS SUPPORT.

I AM MORE THAN GRATEFUL TO KIT HOPKINS FOR ACCOMPANYING ME ON
THIS LONG JOURNEY WHICH WE SOMETIMES THOUGHT WOULD DESTROY US.
IT DIDN'T.

A SPECIAL THANK-YOU TO DONATA AND WIM WENDERS
FOR THEIR FAITH AND INSPIRATION

AMONG OTHER UNNAMED SPONSORS I WOULD LIKE TO THANK WERNER
STAUFFACHER, STÄFA AND FRANK WINKLER, RUESCHLIKON

PRESTEL BOOKS ARE AVAILABLE WORLDWIDE.
PLEASE CONTACT YOUR NEAREST BOOKSELLER OR ONE OF THE FOLLOWING
ADDRESSES FOR INFORMATION CONCERNING YOUR LOCAL DISTRIBUTOR.

PRESTEL VERLAG
KÖNIGINSTRASSE 9, 80539 MUNICH
TEL. +49 (89) 38 17 09-0
FAX +49 (89) 38 17 09-35
WWW.PRESTEL.DE

PRESTEL PUBLISHING LTD.
4, BLOOMSBURY PLACE, LONDON WC1A 2QA
TEL. +44 (020) 7323-5004
FAX +44 (020) 7636-8004

PRESTEL PUBLISHING
175 FIFTH AVENUE, SUITE 402,
NEW YORK, N.Y. 10010
TEL. +1 (212) 995-2720
FAX +1 (212) 995-2733
WWW.PRESTEL.COM

THE LIBRARY OF CONGRESS CATALOGUING-IN-PUBLICATION DATA
IS AVAILABLE.

BRITISH LIBRARY CATALOGUING-IN-PUBLICATION DATA
A CATALOGUE RECORD FOR THIS BOOK IS AVAILABLE FROM
THE BRITISH LIBRARY.

THE DEUTSCHE BIBLIOTHEK HOLDS A RECORD OF THIS
PUBLICATION IN THE DEUTSCHE NATIONALBIBLIOGRAPHIE;
DETAILED BIBLIOGRAPHICAL DATA CAN BE FOUND UNDER:
HTTP://DNB.DDE.DE

EDITORIAL DIRECTION — PETER STEPAN
EDITORS — CHRISTOPHER WYNNE (ENGLISH),
MARTINE PASSELAIGUE (FRENCH)
PRODUCTION AT PRESTEL — MEIKE SELLIER
ORIGINATION, PRINTING AND BINDING — FOTOLITO LONGO, BOLZANO
PRINTED IN GERMANY ON ACID-FREE PAPER